Writing and Civilization: From Ancient Worlds to Modernity

Marc Zender, Ph.D.

PUBLISHED BY:

THE GREAT COURSES
Corporate Headquarters
4840 Westfields Boulevard, Suite 500
Chantilly, Virginia 20151-2299
Phone: 1-800-832-2412
Fax: 703-378-3819
www.thegreatcourses.com

Marc Zender, Ph.D.

Visiting Assistant Professor of Anthropology
Tulane University

Professor Marc Zender is a Visiting Assistant Professor of Anthropology at Tulane University and a Research Associate in Harvard University's Corpus of Maya Hieroglyphic Inscriptions Program. He received an Honors B.A. in Anthropology from The University of British Columbia and an M.A. and a Ph.D. in Archaeology from the University of Calgary.

Professor Zender's M.A. thesis on the orthographic conventions of Mayan hieroglyphic writing won the Governor General's Gold Medal in 1999, and his Ph.D. thesis on Classic Maya priesthood is widely cited in his field. As a Postdoctoral Fellow and Lecturer on Anthropology at Harvard University from 2004 to 2011, Professor Zender taught numerous popular courses. During that period, he was a seven-time recipient of the Harvard University Certificate of Distinction in Teaching, awarded by the Derek Bok Center for Teaching and Learning. He also received the distinguished Petra T. Shattuck Excellence in Teaching Award in 2008.

Professor Zender has published extensively on Mesoamerican languages and writing systems, especially those of the Maya and Aztecs (Nahuatl). His research and teaching interests include anthropological and historical linguistics; decipherment, comparative writing systems, and the origins of writing; and iconography, art, and visual culture. He has done archaeological and epigraphic fieldwork throughout Mexico and Central America and currently works as an epigrapher for both the Belize Valley Archaeological Reconnaissance Project in Belize and the Proyecto arqueológico de Comalcalco in Tabasco, Mexico.

Professor Zender is the coauthor (with Andrea Stone) of *Reading Maya Art: A Hieroglyphic Guide to Ancient Maya Painting and Sculpture*, and he has written numerous journal articles, book chapters, and review essays on Mayan and Aztec hieroglyphic writing. He is the Director of Precolumbia Mesoweb Press, an associate editor of *The PARI Journal* (a publication of the Precolumbian Art Research Institute), and a contributing editor to *Mesoweb*, a major Internet resource for the study of Classic Mayan civilization. Professor Zender is also a talented illustrator; his drawings are featured throughout this course and appear in many books by his colleagues. Committed to spreading popular awareness of his field, Professor Zender gives frequent international workshops on decipherment, and his research has been featured in several documentaries on The History Channel and by the BBC. ■

Table of Contents

Table of Contents

Table of Contents

SUPPLEMENTAL MATERIAL

Typographical Conventions

This guidebook uses the following typographical conventions:

- Italics are used for words cited as words rather than used functionally (e.g., Over time, the pronunciation of the English word *knight* has undergone numerous changes) and for foreign-language words.

- Boldface, lowercase type is used for phonetic signs (e.g., Egyptian **n**, Mayan **na**, Sumerian **a**).

- Boldface, uppercase type is used for logograms (e.g., **BAHLAM**).

- Boldface, italicized type is used for terms that are included in the guidebook's Glossary (e.g., ***abbreviation***).

- Brackets are used to represent phones, that is, speech sounds capable of being made by humans (e.g., [p], representing a voiceless bilabial plosive).

- Forward slashes are used to represent phonemes, that is, speech sounds that are meaningfully used in any given language (e.g., /p/, which can be pronounced either [p] or [pʰ] in English, depending on the context).

- Capital letters are used for Semitic consonantal roots (e.g., Arabic KTB, "writing," Hebrew RB, "master") and semantic signs (e.g., TIME, FEMALE, SWORD).

- A colon (:) following a vowel indicates that the vowel is long (in the linguistic sense of being pronounced for about twice as long, not in the popular sense of "saying its own name"). Some languages conventionally double the vowel to signal this (e.g., *aa*); others add a macron over the vowel (e.g., *ā*). Because this course deals with dozens of languages, it's important to remember that [a:], *aa*, and *ā* are equivalent for our purposes.

- Double quotation marks are used for direct quotations, meanings of words (e.g., The Maya referred to their writing as *k'uhul wooj*, meaning "holy signs"), translations of sentences, and words used in a special sense (e.g., What we might think of as the "Chinese language" is, in fact, eight mutually unintelligible regional languages).

Writing and Civilization:
From Ancient Worlds to Modernity

Scope:

Few human inventions are as pervasive and central to our modern world as writing. Each and every day, most of us read thousands of words, whether in traditional formats, such as books, magazines, or newspapers, or on the increasingly common computers, smartphones, e-book readers, and tablets. But even though writing now seems thoroughly modern, it can be traced back more than 5,000 years to ancient Egypt and Mesopotamia.

This course will begin with a consideration of what writing is and precisely how it differs from other kinds of graphic communication systems. Writing always records language, and it does so in surprisingly similar ways in all writing systems, ancient and modern. The way the ancients wrote millennia ago is not radically different from how we write today.

We will then turn to an exploration of the origins and development of writing, tracing the birth of our own alphabet and its connections to the early Germanic runes. We will also explore the independent invention of writing in China and its adoption and elaboration in Japan.

In order to more deeply examine the subject of writing, we will closely examine the theory and practice of decipherment. Not all writing systems can be deciphered, but what are the limitations, and how can they be overcome? We will explore several case studies to put decipherment to the test, including ancient Egyptian hieroglyphics, Old Persian cuneiform, Mycenaean Linear B, Mayan script, and Aztec hieroglyphs. Once we have studied these and other ancient writing systems, you will know why Etruscan and Meroïtic have proven impossible to decipher; you will understand the urge that numerous individuals have had to reform writing or to invent a more perfect writing system; and you will be able to assess Darius the Great's claim that he himself invented the Old Persian script.

In comparing the world's writing systems, we slip the shackles of parochialism, recognizing that our alphabet is but one of many similar writing systems, all of which capably serve the needs of their users. Writing is deeply conservative and resistant to change. It may undergo adaptation during borrowing, but a culture will never abandon or radically modify its writing system except in the direst instances of cultural transformation through conquest or assimilation. We will also come to understand the deeply interdependent relationship of writing and civilization, including the social, political, and economic forces that led to the adoption of new media and technology for writing. These forces not only shaped the form, function, and distribution of writing, but through it, they have transformed civilization itself. In the concluding lecture, we consider all that we have learned about the interplay between writing and civilization and use it to predict one possible future of writing. ∎

What Is Writing?

Lecture 1

It's almost impossible to imagine a technology more central than writing to the way we live and communicate. We use writing every day, and it's all around us all the time. But precisely because of its ubiquity, we take writing for granted, as if it has always been here and always will be. We should recall, however, that writing was a human invention. At some point in the remote past, some inspired individual or small group first hit on the idea of writing. In this lecture, we'll look at ancient ideas about writing as a divine gift, and we'll arrive at a modern definition of writing to enable us to embark on our comparative study.

A Gift of the Gods

- Some ancient civilizations regarded *writing* as a divine gift. The Egyptians, for example, believed that writing was created by the god of wisdom, Thoth. The Egyptians called their god-given *hieroglyphs* **mdwt nṭr** ("speech of the gods"), a term that Greek historians translated as "hieroglyph," from Greek *hieros* ("sacred") and *glyphē* ("carving").

- In nearby *Mesopotamia*, the ancient Sumerians believed that writing was invented by the head of their pantheon, Énlil. The later Assyrians and Babylonians borrowed their writing from the Sumerians, but they attributed its invention to their own god Nábû.

- In the New World, the Classic Maya of Mexico and Guatemala attributed the invention of writing to their sky god, Itzamnaaj. The Maya referred to their writing as *k'uhul wooj* ("holy signs"); thus, scholars also refer to them as hieroglyphs.

- In the Bible, the books of Exodus and Deuteronomy report that the Ten Commandments were written with "the finger of God" and were set down in "the first writing." In the Book of Daniel, disembodied fingers wrote a cryptic message of doom on the walls of Babylon. These are just two of many biblical stories in which writing serves as a vehicle of divine inspiration or judgment.

The Stability of Writing

- One of the reasons that early writing systems remained stable for so long is precisely because they were sacred. To abandon or alter them would have been sacrilegious. Thus, Egyptian hieroglyphic writing persisted in the same complex mixture of word, sound, and semantic *signs* for more than 3,000 years.

- Updating a writing system may seem like a good idea, especially if the language has changed and the writing system doesn't accurately reflect it, but there are practical reasons for the inertia of writing systems.

Later pharaohs attempted to erase King Tutankhamun from history, but his name and some of his accomplishments are known to us now from the written records left behind in his tomb.

  - Consider the English word *knight*, for instance, with its silent initial *k* and silent internal *gh*. When this spelling first became the standard, the word was pronounced [knixt]. But over time, spoken English lost these sounds, and the word *knight* underwent other changes. It's now pronounced [nait] but still written as if it were pronounced [knixt].

  - Updating such spellings would radically change the appearance of written English and limit access to literature written in Early Modern English, such as the work of Shakespeare or the King James Bible, to all but a few experts.

- An important feature of writing generally is that it allows our names and words to outlive us. Our own tombstones and epitaphs, like those of ancient kings, are designed to recall our names, dates, and cherished family connections for future generations.

- The way we write today is not fundamentally different from the way the Mesopotamians and Egyptians wrote more than 5,000 years ago; this means that we can learn quite a lot about the origins, development, and significance of writing by comparing our own *alphabet* with other writing systems, both ancient and modern.

Defining *Writing*

- In defining words, we often look to dictionaries for help, but in the case of the word *writing*, dictionary definitions are a bit misleading. They are either too general, describing the appearance of writing without concern for its structure, or too specific, focusing on alphabets to the exclusion of other types of writing.
  - For instance, one common dictionary definition of *writing* is "marks (letters, words, or other symbols) inscribed on a surface, often paper, with a suitable implement."

  - This definition captures the form and medium of some writing systems, and it correctly conveys the graphic nature of writing, but it's narrow in its focus on paper, and it's much too vague when it comes to what writing actually is.

- A second common definition of *writing* is "a system of visible marks used to transmit ideas." This meaning seems overly broad. There are many systems of visible marks that can convey ideas and information, including maps, musical notation, mathematical formulas, *pictographic* street signs, and so on.
  - Some scholars argue in favor of a broad definition of writing that includes all forms of graphic communication. But by this definition, the comparative field would be vast, including everything from cave paintings to pictographic street signs. Even art and iconography would become, in this definition, a kind of writing.

○ Such a broad definition seems counterintuitive. Most of us recognize that there are similarities between our own alphabet and Egyptian hieroglyphic writing that simply aren't shared with cave paintings and street signs.

○ For example, both our alphabet and Egyptian have signs for sounds, and those signs convey information only to the extent that they match words in the English and Egyptian languages. Further, the order of these signs has to match the order of the sounds in the language; otherwise, the message is nonsensical. Other graphic communication systems, such as cave paintings and pictography, don't have phonetic signs, don't match the order of spoken words, and don't rely on language at all to transmit information.

• In contrast to pictography—a system of nonlinguistic graphic communication conveying information through imagery and context—writing is a system of graphic marks conveying information through language. It does this by using phonetic signs to communicate the sounds of a language and by putting those signs in an order that reflects the order of elements in the language.

• Nonlinguistic graphic communication systems have no unifying features or structural principles in common. Cave paintings, musical notation, and pictographic street signs just don't form a natural set—not with one another and not with writing.

The Link between Writing and Civilization

• The real motivation for linking nonlinguistic graphic communication systems with writing seems to stem more from empathy and political correctness than from the demands of objective evidence. The connection of the two systems can be traced to the late-19th-century anthropologists Edward Burnett Tylor (1832–1917) and Lewis Henry Morgan (1818–1881) and their unilinear view of cultural evolution.

○ Tylor and Morgan argued that human societies had progressed through several stages of social complexity, which they labeled bands, tribes, chiefdoms, and states. They listed criteria that they saw as characterizing each of these social stages.

○ One of the hallmark traits listed for the state level of social organization was writing. In other words, cultures with a writing system were civilized; cultures without one were uncivilized.

• The anthropologist Franz Boas (1858–1942) systematically dismantled this simplistic view in the early 20th century, pointing out numerous counterexamples to Tylor and Morgan's predictions. He noted that some state-level societies had existed without writing, such as the Inka Empire of South America, and that some band-and tribal-level societies had writing, such as the early-19th-century Cherokee.

• Not everyone recognized Boas's cautious counterexamples. Even later in the 20th century, the founder of the field of ***grammatology***, Ignace Gelb (1907–1985), wrote, "Writing exists only in a civilization and a civilization cannot exist without writing." Boas had already shown that this claim is untrue, but the idea of a one-to-one association between writing and civilization remains popular nonetheless.

• This popular understanding naturally has an impact on our view of such societies as the Inka Empire.
○ Undoubtedly, the Inka Empire was a state-level civilization, with elaborate roads and other infrastructure, complex administration, and remarkable territorial extent and control over subject provinces.

○ The Inka also had a system of intricately knotted and colored cords known as khipu that could be used to keep track of information about goods and labor. Khipu are fascinating objects, but no one has ever been able to demonstrate that they record language.

- There is certainly a strong connection between writing and civilization, but it's not a simple cause-and-effect relationship. Rather, writing is a tool for, and a product of, numerous important social structures, such as religion, politics, and economy, and it's in a complex feedback relationship with these same social structures.

Writing as Visible Speech

- To return to the definition of *writing*, specialists now divide nonlinguistic graphic communication systems from writing proper. In this course, we will follow a definition of writing first proposed by the linguist Archibald Hill (1886–1977) and later refined by John DeFrancis (1911–2009), a scholar of Chinese writing.

- As Hill noted in 1967, "all writing represents speech." Much more recently, DeFrancis put it similarly: "writing is visible speech." Both scholars would agree that writing is a system of graphic marks representing the sounds and words of spoken language. As we've seen, this definition is also intuitively satisfying in that it recognizes the fact that different kinds of writing are similar to one another in this way.

- DeFrancis also said that there is a "diverse oneness of writing." The use of phonetic signs to record spoken language is a hallmark of writing systems. A pattern of striking simplicity underlies the superficial differences of all writing systems, past and present, knitting them together into a coherent whole. All writing systems have phonetic signs, and all writing systems link symbols together in an order dictated by the language being represented.

- When we compare writing systems using the definition of writing as "visible speech," we open up a fascinating world of discovery.
  - Writing systems are intrinsically interesting as beautiful and mysterious inventions stretching back beyond the beginnings of recorded history.

  - A comparative study of writing also teaches us things about past cultures and languages that we can't learn any other way.

    ○   Further, the study of superficially different but structurally similar scripts is a cure for our own parochialism, opening our eyes to other possibilities and shedding light on the tensions between innovative and conservative forces in our own culture, language, and writing system. Through these lectures, we'll not only learn about ancient writing systems and civilizations but also about ourselves.

Important Terms

alphabet: A writing system composed of a mixture of consonantal and vocalic signs.

grammatology: The comparative study of writing systems. The term was coined by Ignace Gelb (1952). A student of comparative writing is a grammatologist.

hieroglyph: Literally "sacred carving" (from Greek); now refers to single signs in a hieroglyphic script. Initially applied only to Egyptian but now freely used to describe many pictorial logophonetic scripts, such as Hittite (Luwian), Mayan, and Aztec.

Mesopotamia: The land between the Tigris and Euphrates rivers in present-day Iraq; a rich alluvial plain sometimes called the "fertile crescent." Mesopotamia was the site of the ancient civilizations of Akkad, Assyria, Babylonia, Elam, and Sumer.

pictography (also **picture writing**): A system of nonlinguistic graphic communication conveying information through imagery and context. Most writing systems have signs that originated pictographically, but this says nothing about the function of those signs in a writing system, which will always be phonetic, logographic, or semantic. Grammatologists have retired the term *pictogram* (or *pictograph*) as a sign type.

sign (or **grapheme**): An irreducible graphic unit of a script possessing its own reading value. The major sign types are logograms, phonetic signs, semantic signs, diacritics, and numerals.

writing: A system of graphic marks representing the sounds and words of spoken language. As DeFrancis noted: "writing is visible speech."

Suggested Reading

Boone and Mignolo, *Writing without Words*.

DeFrancis, *Visible Speech*.

Gelb, *A Study of Writing*.

Hill, "The Typology of Writing Systems."

Mallery, *Pictographs of the North American Indians*.

Mann, "Cracking the Khipu Code."

Polacco, *Thank You, Mr. Falker*.

Urton, *Signs of the Inka Khipu*.

Urton and Brezine, "Khipu Accounting in Ancient Peru."

Wells, *A Short History of the World*.

Questions to Consider

1. Take a moment to consider how often you read or write during a typical day. How would your life be transformed if there was no such thing as writing?

2. Why is it important that we define *writing* as "visible speech"? How is writing different from the symbols on restroom doors?

3. Why do you suppose writing was so often regarded as a gift of the gods?

4. What is meant by the term *hieroglyph* (or *hieroglyphic*)? Do you find it confusing that the same term is used for scripts as different from one another as Egyptian, Meroïtic, Mayan, and Aztec? Confusing or not, is the usage appropriate? Come back to this question periodically as you complete more lectures in this course.

The Origins and Development of Writing
Lecture 2

In this lecture, we explore three myths about where writing comes from and how it developed. The first of these is that writing was invented only once, after which it was borrowed by later groups. The second myth is that writing began with clay tokens, considered the forerunners of pictorial signs for sheep, grain, oil, and so on. The idea here is that once the idea of impressing shapes into clay caught hold, the tokens themselves were abandoned, and writing emerged. The third myth is that writing was developed to serve the administrative needs of early cities; in other words, writing was invented by history's first accountants. As we'll see in this lecture, none of these beliefs is true.

Monogenesis: The Theory of "Single Origin"

- The theory that writing was invented only once and then borrowed by later groups is called *monogenesis*. Although this idea remains popular, scientific comparison clearly shows that it can't be true. For example, there is now no doubt that *Mayan* hieroglyphic writing and other ancient writing systems of Mexico developed independently of those in the Old World.

- What about Old World writing systems? Could they have descended from one original script? Some scholars would place this origin in Mesopotamia; others, in Egypt. In both of these regions, evidence of writing is found by at least 3100 B.C.

- The Egyptian and Mesopotamian civilizations are remarkably close neighbors, which is the main reason that their writing systems are often thought to be related. In the 19th century, the idea that something as complex and ingenious as writing could have been independently invented in multiple places seemed absurd. Outright borrowing, or at least borrowing of the idea of writing, seemed more likely.

- To test this theory, we can look to later writing systems that we know were borrowed to discover certain structural hallmarks of borrowing.

  o The most famous example of a borrowed writing system is Japanese writing, which was adapted from Chinese writing in the 5th century A.D. Japanese signs contain clear indications of having been borrowed from China, including shared sign shapes, reading values, and spelling rules.

  o The *cuneiform* scripts also represent more than a dozen cases of borrowing. As with Chinese signs in Japanese writing, the borrowed scripts provide internal evidence for their origins, including shared sign shapes, reading values, and spelling rules. Scholars can use these features to trace a borrowed script, such as Hittite cuneiform, back to its source, in this instance, Akkadian cuneiform.

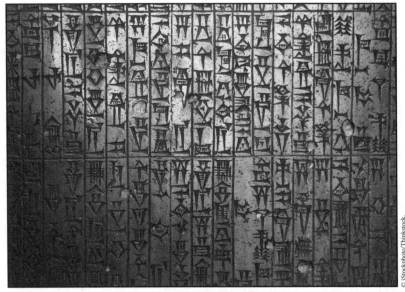

© iStockphoto/Thinkstock.

Even in cases where certain cuneiform scripts were not borrowed directly from precursor scripts but were merely inspired by them, the form and arrangement of these scripts still indicate their derivative nature.

- As a final example, consider the origins of our own alphabet. Most people know that we can trace it back to the Romans. But the Romans borrowed their alphabet from the Etruscans, who had borrowed it from the Greeks in the 8ᵗʰ century B.C. The Greeks, in turn, had borrowed their alphabet from the Phoenicians, who had borrowed their script from **Proto-Sinaitic**, which dates back to almost 2000 B.C.

- We can follow the development of the alphabet in the case of our own letter *A*. The arbitrary shape of the letter *A* goes all the way back to Greece, where *alpha* was the name of the first letter of the alphabet. Why this name, and why the shape of the letter?

- The Greek letter *alpha* was rotated 90 degrees from its original orientation in Phoenician script, where it was used for a **glottal** stop **consonant**.

- The letter *A* actually began as a picture of an ox's head (Hebrew **'aleph**), and it was clearly intended to conjure up the first sound in the **Semitic** word *'aleph* ("ox"), namely, a glottal stop.

- When Greek speakers borrowed the Phoenician alphabet, they didn't need the glottal stop sound; thus, they ignored the initial glottal stop of the word *'aleph* and called the sign *alpha*, using it for the sound [a], which was basically the first sound they heard in the Semitic word.

- Are there any shared structural features between Egyptian or Sumerian that would suggest borrowing? The answer is no. Egyptian and Sumerian resemble each other only insofar as their signs have pictorial origins. There are no shared sign forms, sound values, or spelling rules.

- There is also no linking narrative between these systems, such as the story we can tell about the letter *A*. Similarly, when we compare the early writing systems of Minoan Crete, China, and Mexico to those of Egypt and Mesopotamia, we find that none of these writing systems has the kinds of similarities we see between truly related scripts.

- It's still too early to rule out all contacts between these writing systems, but the available evidence now suggests that writing was invented independently around the world on at least five different occasions.
  - o Apart from at least five independent inventions of writing, nearly all other writing systems appear to have been borrowed. This includes all of the world's alphabets (ancient and modern) and most of the cuneiform scripts.

  - o It's important to note that an important feature of borrowing is innovation. Writing is never borrowed without some invention, elaboration, or alteration. Scholars call this process "borrowing with adaptation."

Writing Inspired by Clay Tokens
- The theory that writing was inspired by clay tokens used in accounting was proposed by the archaeologist Denise Schmandt-Besserat. Although this theory remains popular, it's not widely accepted by specialists of comparative writing.

- The chronological correlation of clay tokens with the first writing is difficult to explain if tokens truly gave rise to writing. Tokens preceded writing in Mesopotamia by almost 5,000 years, and they continued to exist alongside writing for more than 1,500 years. The pattern suggests two independent systems perhaps serving different functions.

- Further, if different shapes of tokens were actually the forerunners of pictorial signs, we might expect some formal correlation between tokens and the earliest signs. But apart from a few possibly coincidental resemblances, there is no strong correlation.

- Comparative evidence also compels us to ask why tokens are limited to early Mesopotamia if writing developed independently several times in different parts of the world.
  - When scholars still supported script monogenesis, it was fine to point to tokens in Mesopotamia as the origin for all writing, but now, the use of tokens seems like a purely local phenomenon.

  - What we need to explain is why at least five different ancient civilizations independently hit on phonetic signs as the core of their inventions of writing. Seen in this light, the long focus on clay tokens in discussions of the invention of writing is a category error.

Writing for Administrative Requirements

- It's true that some of the earliest clay tablets from Mesopotamia, dating from the late 4th millennium B.C., record transactions involving barley. It's also true that bureaucratic palace records were the entire output of Mycenaean *Linear B* (the ancient writing system of Crete), and the same thing seems to be true of the older, undeciphered *Linear A* inscriptions. But when we move away from the Mesopotamian and Cretan examples, we find numerous counterexamples to the claim that writing was developed for purely administrative purposes.

- For example, the first writing in China, represented by the Shang oracle bones of 1200 B.C., has much to say about divination and religious ritual but almost nothing about ancient economy. Similarly, the earliest writing systems in Mesoamerica and Egypt were used for political functions: to record the names and titles of royalty in *captions* associated with figural art. Writing also appeared in "nametags"—labels recording the private ownership of treasured objects. Thus, early writing appears to have been used for a fairly heterogeneous set of purposes.

- Again, we have to ask why the administrative use of early writing appears limited to Mesopotamia and Crete. Given that writing apparently developed independently several times in different parts of the world and was used for multiple purposes, we are better off discarding administration as a prime mover. When scholars still supported the idea of script monogenesis, Mesopotamian administration seemed to be a reasonable model, but once again, we now have to consider the origins of writing more broadly.

Recording Proper Nouns

- Writing is an eminently adaptable technology. For this reason, our best hope for uncovering its origins is to study its structural characteristics. As we noted in the last lecture, writing is visible speech, making use of phonetic signs to record language. Phoneticism is also the structural hallmark of at least five independent inventions of writing and characterizes all later borrowings and adaptations of writing. Why should this be so?

- Quite unlike the *numerals*, icons, heraldic emblems, and magical sigils that would have been sufficient for the purposes often imagined as having given rise to writing, there is one category of spoken language not so amendable to symbolic representation. That category is the *proper noun*.
  - ○ From a comparative perspective, proper nouns are highly language specific and resist translation. There are some proper nouns that still bear meaning, but they are in fairly short supply.

  - ○ Where obvious meanings have been lost, the only way to record such names is with phonetic signs, just as we do in our alphabet and as the Egyptians and Aztecs did with the names of foreign conquerors from Greece and Spain, respectively. This is why phonetic signs are already present in the earliest known writing systems.

  - ○ In the first writing from Egypt and Mesopotamia, we already find personal names and titles. Both of these scripts routinely caption images with names, as do the New World scripts. And all writing systems label important objects with the names of their owners.

- The specific use of writing to label ownership of objects might be secondary to the original use of writing, but the larger point is inescapable: Phonetic signs are the hallmark of writing, and it's their presence we have to explain if we want to understand the invention of writing. The most reasonable explanation of the development of phonetic signs is that they were needed to write categories of words that could not easily be written in any other way. Proper names, in whatever environment, are the prime candidates.

- Writing was independently invented several times in human history. It's not related to clay tokens, and although it's useful for accounting, it's equally useful for pretty much everything else! Writing seems to have grown out of a need to record proper nouns, but once it was invented, it proved itself the most adaptable of tools, eminently suited to all kinds of purposes, and an irresistible lure to all who came into contact with it, borrowing and adapting it to their own languages and purposes.

Important Terms

'aleph: The first letter of the Hebrew alphabet, representing a glottal plosive consonant ([ʔ]). The Hebrew sign derives from Proto-Sinaitic, where it depicts an ox (Semitic: *'ālp*).

caption: A short text adjacent to an illustrated figure or object, which it names or describes.

consonant: A speech sound in which the breath is at least partly obstructed and which cannot form the nucleus of a syllable on its own (e.g., *p*).

cuneiform: Any of a large group of Near Eastern writing systems having wedge-shaped characters. Some of these scripts are historically related (e.g., Sumerian, Babylonian, and Hittite); others are merely visually influenced by them (e.g., Ugaritic, Old Persian).

glottal: Refers to a sound made with the glottis (the part of the larynx consisting of the vocal cords and the slitlike opening between them), such as fricative [h] and plosive [ʔ] (Hebrew *'aleph*).

Linear A: An undeciphered logosyllabic script found mostly on Crete, Thera, and other Cycladic islands, dating to c. 1800–1450 B.C.

Linear B (also **Mycenaean script**): Logosyllabic script recording the Mycenaean Greek language, mostly known from Crete and mainland Greece and dating to c. 1450–1200 B.C. Deciphered by Michael Ventris in 1952.

Mayan: Refers to a large group of related languages and their speakers in Mexico and Central America. By convention, *Maya* refers to the people and their culture, whereas *Mayan* specifically refers to language.

monogenesis: The theory that writing was invented only once (usually in Mesopotamia), after which it diffused to all later groups.

numeral (or **numeric sign**): A sign for a number, such as the Arabic numerals 1, 2, and 3.

proper name (also **proper noun** or **rigid designator**): A name used for a specific person, place, or thing. In English, proper names always receive initial capital letters.

Proto-Sinaitic: The oldest known ancestor of the alphabet, a pictorial abjad (writing system that comprises consonantal signs only) dating to the mid-19th century B.C. and currently attested in the southwest Sinai Peninsula and Middle Egypt.

Semitic: A large family of languages spoken in the Middle East and Ethiopia, including Arabic, Hebrew, Aramaic, and the now-extinct Babylonian. Best known for its three-consonant word roots, e.g., Arabic KTB ("write"), giving *kataba* ("he wrote"), *maktab* ("office"), and so on. The common ancestor of these languages is known as Proto-Semitic.

Suggested Reading

Christin, ed., *Histoire de l'écriture*.

Gelb, *A Study of Writing*.

Houston, ed., *The Shape of Script*.

Oates, ed., *World Archaeology* (Special issue: Early Writing Systems).

Schmandt-Besserat, *Before Writing*.

Questions to Consider

1. Other than the ones mentioned in this lecture, can you think of any other myths about ancient scripts or the origins of writing? Why do you suppose these myths remain popular?

2. How attached do you feel to your personal name? Are you at all uncomfortable when people spell or pronounce it wrong? Do you mind if they shorten it without asking?

Where Did Our Alphabet Come From?
Lecture 3

Most people know that our alphabet is technically referred to as the Roman (or Latin) alphabet. It initially spread during the days of the Roman Republic and continued during the Roman imperial period and the medieval Holy Roman Empire. As a result of the vast military power, socioeconomic influence, and religious authority of Rome, derivatives of the Roman alphabet are now used to write hundreds of modern languages. Not coincidentally, these languages include those of the great colonial powers of the last half millennium: English, Dutch, Spanish, Portuguese, and French. In this lecture, we'll investigate the development of the alphabet and explore some fascinating recent discoveries about its origins.

Connected Alphabets
- Dozens of alphabets are in daily use around the world today, and all but a handful are connected by borrowing from a single invention almost 4,000 years ago.
    - The early Germanic peoples adapted the early Roman alphabet into the runic alphabet in the 2nd century A.D., and English itself was first written in runes. Centuries later, English speakers again borrowed the Roman alphabet, replacing their runic script with it.

    - Another connected script is the Greek alphabet, which was passed to the Etruscans, who in turn passed it to the Romans.

    - The Greek alphabet was also developed into the *Cyrillic* alphabet. Cyrillic is now used to write Russian, Bulgarian, Serbian, and Ukrainian, as well as other Slavic languages.

    - The modern Arabic and Hebrew scripts are also connected to our alphabet, though the Phoenician script that gave rise to them hasn't survived.

- o Even Braille, Morse code, and American Sign Language trace their origins to the alphabet. They may not use linear signs, but their order and arrangement are copied from the alphabet.

- The connections between the widely shared alphabets include not only the shapes of signs and their phonetic values but also their organization.
  - o Thus, the order of letters in our alphabet (*a*, *b*, *c*, ...) is not appreciably different from the order of letters used by the Romans, Greeks, and Phoenicians.

  - o A vestige of this shared order even survives in the word *alphabet*, which comes from Late Latin *alphabetum*. This word, in turn, comes from Greek *alphabetos*, in reference to the first two letters of the Greek alphabet: *alpha* and *beta*.

The Phoenician Alphabet

- Similarities in the shapes, sounds, and organization of the alphabet have been recognized for centuries. Writing in the 5th century B.C., the historian Herodotus correctly traced the origins of Greek letters to the Phoenicians.

- The link to the Phoenicians is both logical and likely. Phoenicia was a major trading power in the Mediterranean during the early part of the 1st millennium B.C.
  - o The Phoenician homeland (or ancient Canaan) was located on the shores of the eastern Mediterranean Sea, roughly corresponding to modern Lebanon, the coastal plains of Syria, and Palestine.

  - o At the height of their influence, Phoenician traders reached all the shores of the Mediterranean, and Phoenician colonists settled much of the southwestern Mediterranean, including Tunisia, Morocco, and Algeria, as well as Malta, Sicily, and even Spain.

o Perhaps the most valuable commodity the Phoenicians brought into the Mediterranean was their writing system.

• The Phoenician script of 22 letters was technically an ***abjad***, which means that it recorded consonants only, not ***vowels***. Such a system seems a bit odd to us, but Semitic languages are structured in such a way that consonants are much more important than vowels.

o The Arabic root KTB, meaning "write," is a favorite example. Such roots must be fleshed out with vowels to form words. Thus, the basic meaning of "write" is derived by certain patterns of vowels to produce various verbs and nouns related to writing: *katab*, "to write"; *kitaab*, "book"; and *maktaba*, "library."

o Common to all of these words is the consonantal root KTB, whereas English requires different root words, such as *write*, *book*, and *library*, to translate the Arabic forms.

• In a language in which consonants convey meaning and vowels are often predictable from context, it naturally makes sense for the writing system to highlight consonants at the expense of vowels. This explains why this feature of the Phoenician script has been retained by descendant scripts used to write other Semitic languages, such as Aramaic, Hebrew, and Arabic, all of which use the same consonantal root system.

Greek Adaptations

• The Greeks who adopted the Phoenician script in about 900 B.C. did not speak a Semitic language but an ***Indo-European*** one. Like other Indo-European languages, Greek required vowels to signal the grammatical endings of its rich inflectional system.

• Rather than inventing new signs for vowels, the Greeks followed the common practice of adapting existing signs to their needs. Given the profound differences between Semitic and Indo-European languages, there were actually a fair number of sounds in Phoenician that the Greek didn't have, and the signs for these sounds could be altered to serve the needs of written Greek.

o Most notably, this adaptation included the first letter of the Phoenician abjad, the *'aleph* sign, which signaled a glottal stop consonant.

o The Greeks didn't even hear this sound and simply adapted the letter *'aleph* (which they came to call *alpha*) to write the vowel sound [aː]. They made similar adaptations throughout the system, thereby converting the Semitic abjad into an alphabet.

- Apart from the phonetic substitutions, there is another striking feature we notice only when we compare the Greek and Phoenician sign forms: The Greek forms are all rotated by varying degrees. Scholars still aren't entirely sure why some signs were rotated and others were not.

Discoveries at Serabit

- Scholars of the late 19th century had already identified most of these connections between Greek and Phoenician, and it was generally assumed that the Phoenicians had, in fact, invented the alphabet they ended up broadcasting across the Mediterranean. That changed in 1905 with a series of discoveries made by Hilda Petrie (1871–1956), wife of the Egyptologist Sir Flinders Petrie (1853–1942).

- The Petries were excavating at Serabit el-Khadim, a mountain in the southwest Sinai Peninsula. There, Hilda Petrie noticed graffiti in a temple to the Egyptian goddess Hathor (dating to the beginning of the 2nd millennium B.C.) and in nearby turquoise mines. The graffiti was written using 22 pictorial signs. Given the small number of signs and their frequent repetition, this script was obviously an alphabet or abjad, but interpretation of it proved difficult.

- In 1916, the Egyptologist Sir Alan Gardiner noted a frequently repeated set of four signs, which he interpreted as the letters **b-'-l-t**, recording the Canaanite appellative *Ba'alat*, "Lady." The key to his interpretation was a bilingual inscription on a small stone sphinx

Turquoise mines at Serabit el-Khadim had been worked by Egyptian expeditions for hundreds of years and yielded interesting incised graffiti in the early 20ᵗʰ century.

from the temple to Hathor. The Egyptian hieroglyphic inscription on the sphinx could be read as "Beloved of Hathor, Lady of Turquoise." This phrase was associated with a text of seven signs in the pictorial alphabet.

- ○ Gardiner speculated that the presence of Canaanites at Serabit might explain these seven signs and that they perhaps recorded a Semitic language in an early abjad.

- ○ He compared some of the signs to likely candidates in Semitic vocabulary and sign shapes in the Phoenician, Aramaic, Arabic, and Hebrew scripts. He eventually proposed that the signs be transcribed as **m-'-h-(b) b-'-l-t** and read as "Beloved of the Lady," a reasonable translation of Egyptian "Beloved of Hathor, Lady of Turquoise."

- • Gardiner's decipherment has been well received, though other inscriptions at Serabit have proven more difficult to translate, and not all scholars agree on the precise reading of all the signs or the mechanisms by which this pictorial script originated.

Recent Discoveries

- About 10 years ago, a dramatic find in Middle Egypt threw the Sinai origin of this script into question. In the summer of 1993–1994, the Egyptologists John and Deborah Darnell were surveying the desert roads that once linked the ancient cities of Thebes and Abydos to important settlements. In a derelict ravine known as Wadi el-Ḥôl ("Ravine of Terror"), the Darnells discovered two graffiti that were strikingly similar to those discovered by the Petries at Serabit el-Khadim.

- The Wadi el-Ḥôl inscriptions have been recorded and studied by Bruce Zuckerman, a scholar of West Semitic inscriptions. Like the Serabit inscriptions, frustratingly little can be made out for certain, but both the "ox" (*'aleph*) and "house" (*beth*) signs can be seen.

- The association with Egyptian texts at the same site suggests a date somewhere around 1900 B.C. The probable Semitic vocabulary, coupled with the connection to the earlier Serabit el-Khadim finds, suggests that these inscriptions were made by Semitic speakers traveling through the region with Egyptians, perhaps as mercenaries in Egyptian armies or as merchants.

- At the end of the day, we know much less than we'd like to about this early abjad, the origin of our own alphabet. Scholars still hope for more texts, preferably bilingual inscriptions, to increase our certainty about the values of these early signs and to test Gardiner's "alphabet hypothesis."

Development by the Canaanites

- By the early 18th century B.C., Canaanite immigrants had founded the large city of Avaris (Tell el-Dab'a) in the eastern Nile delta. In less than 200 years, they would conquer and rule Egypt for a time as the Hyksos. Sometime in the period between their arrival and conquest, during their first acculturation to Egyptian civilization, some of the Canaanites may have invented what would become the alphabet.

- Surrounded by several Egyptian scripts, it's little wonder that they recognized the utility of writing or that they chose a pictorial script as the proper vehicle of language. Seen in this light, choosing the head of an ox to represent the first sound in the word *'aleph* seems a natural solution. This process is called ***acrophony***, and as we will see throughout these lectures, it is common in the world's writing systems.

- Still debated, however, is the extent to which Egyptian hieroglyphs formed a model for the new script. Apart from the proximity of the two scripts and their shared pictorial nature, none of the early alphabetic signs looks much like contemporary Egyptian ones, nor do they share any sound values. It's perhaps safest to regard the early Canaanite abjad as having been inspired by Egyptian literacy but not directly derived from it.

- Over time, as the Canaanite script was adopted and adapted by speakers of other Semitic languages, it became stylized and simplified, losing its pictorial character in favor of more linear forms.

- The simplicity of the alphabet, allowing it to be easily transmitted in even a short period of time, is undoubtedly a factor in its popularity. With the addition of vowels (courtesy of its adaptation by the Greeks), the alphabet is also capable of reasonably recording practically any language.

Important Terms

abjad (or **consonantary**): A writing system composed of consonantal signs only, such as Proto-Sinaitic and Phoenician. The term was coined by Peter Daniels (1990).

acrophony: Process whereby a phonetic sign originates from the initial sounds of a logogram.

Cyrillic: A Greek-derived alphabet named after the late-9th-century Greek missionary Saint Cyril and now used to write Russian, Ukrainian, and other Slavic languages.

Indo-European: The large language family now occupying most of Europe, Iran, and India and including English, Latin, Greek, and Sanskrit. The common ancestor of these languages probably originated on the northern steppes of the Black Sea and is known as Proto-Indo-European.

vowel: A speech sound produced by a relatively open vocal tract, with vibration of the vocal cords but without audible friction. Usually forms the nucleus of a syllable. Depending on where they are made in the mouth, vowels can be classified as high (*i*, *u*), mid (*e*, *o*), low (*a*), front (*e*, *i*), and back (*o*, *u*). Thus, *i* is high front vowel; *o* a mid back one.

Suggested Reading

Bodel, "Paragrams, Punctuation, and System in Ancient Roman Script."

Bonfante, *Etruscan*.

Cook, *Greek Inscriptions*.

Darnell et al., "Two Early Alphabetic Inscriptions from the Wadi el-Ḥôl."

Diringer, *The Alphabet*.

Goldwasser, "How the Alphabet Was Born from Hieroglyphs."

Sacks, *Language Visible*.

Sandys, *Latin Epigraphy*.

Wilford, "Finds in Egypt Date Alphabet in Earlier Era."

1. Is there sufficient evidence in the two widely spaced occurrences of Proto-Sinaitic inscriptions (at Serabit el-Khadim and Wadi el-Ḥôl) for scholars to presume a widespread tradition of writing in this system? Why or why not? What would it take to change your impression?

2. Try writing out some English sentences without representing any of the vowels, then pass them to someone else to read. This approximates how early abjads, such as Proto-Sinaitic and Phoenician, were written. How hard is it to understand English without vowels?

The Fuþark—A Germanic Alphabet
Lecture 4

It's often thought that the German barbarians of northern Europe were first taught to read and write by 7th-century Christian missionaries, but in fact, the Germanic tribes had learned to write at least 500 years earlier. They had an alphabet called runic, derived from the Roman alphabet. The peoples of Britain, Scandinavia, and northwestern Europe all wrote in runes until this system was replaced by still another Roman-derived alphabet, the script English speakers still use today. Unlike many other writing systems, runes never needed to be deciphered and could easily have remained with us. In this lecture, we'll look at the real history of this alphabet as a case study in why writing systems rise and fall.

Derivation from the Roman Alphabet

- The earliest *runes* found date to the mid-2nd century A.D.; thus, they developed during a time when the cultural influence of Rome was at its height. One scholar in particular, Henrik Williams, has done a remarkable job of highlighting just how strong the evidence is for the derivation of runes from the Roman alphabet. The time and region of the earliest runes, as well as their shapes and sound values, all point inexorably to the Roman alphabet as their source.

  ○ Several runes look almost exactly like letters of the Roman alphabet. For example, the first letter of the runic alphabet is a sign that not only looks like but also represents the same sound as the Roman letter *F*.

  ○ Still other runes seem mysterious. For instance, the rune shaped most like a Roman *P* represents the sound /w/, whereas the actual rune for the sound /p/ looks nothing like the Roman *P* or, for that matter, any Roman letter.

  ○ Despite such mysteries and uncertainties, the basic derivation of runes from the Roman alphabet can't be doubted.

- The barbarian tribes who lived at the northern fringes of the Roman Empire spoke a language that scholars now call *Germanic*. This label is used to identify a large group of closely related languages spoken in northwestern Europe by the ancestors of such groups as the Goths, Vandals, Lombards, Franks, and so on.

- Like most tribal peoples in contact with a complex urban civilization (and its military), the Germanic peoples were overwhelmed by the Roman Empire.
  - Conquered Germanic leaders had to give up their sons to the Romans, who were then held captive in Rome or at various frontier garrisons. Of course, while they were captive, they learned something of the ways of their captors.

  - Young Germanic men also served in Roman armies, and we know that Roman legionaries were taught the rudiments of the Roman alphabet, including how to sign their names. This would have provided another mechanism for Germanic speakers to be introduced to the early Roman alphabet.

  - Letters sent to the Roman frontier in northern England during the 1st and 2nd centuries A.D. may also have served as the source and inspiration for runes.

- Whether it was a Germanic-speaking legionary returning home after his time in the army or a Romanized Germanic prince returning from captivity to succeed his father, it seems clear that at least some familiarity with Roman letters preceded the invention of runes. Most importantly, of the 24 runes used in the earliest runic script, more than half of them can now be shown to derive directly from the Roman alphabet in terms of shape and sound value.

Rune Sticks

- The earliest runic alphabet is known as the fuþark, after the sound values of the first six runes. Most of the signs have one or more full-length vertical lines, called staves, that sprout diagonal branches. Note that runes do not have horizontal lines.

- The long staves of runes were designed to be cut perpendicularly across wood grain. Any horizontal lines, which would have to run parallel with the grain, would lack contrast or even be indistinguishable.

- The early focus on cutting signs into wood is probably reflected in our word *writing*, which comes from Old English *writan*, properly meaning "to inscribe" and "to engrave." In copying Roman alphabetic letters (mostly painted or inked on vellum), the early Germanic rune carvers had to make several formal concessions to the medium of carving on wood. This served to hide the derivation of runes from Roman letters for a long time.

- The archaeological record backs up this formal analysis. Rune-inscribed sticks are well described in Viking sagas and early historical sources. But some scholars wondered how accurate these descriptions were, believing that runes might not have been quite so versatile at communicating language as the sources described.

- Those beliefs changed in 1955, when a great fire ravaged the historic district of Bergen, Norway. Archaeologists seized the opportunity to dig below the foundations of the modern city to the medieval seaport below. There, in layers dating back to the 12th century A.D., more than 500 rune-inscribed wooden objects were found.
    - Many of these objects are rune sticks that could be attached to belongings or stuck into bales of goods to identify their owners.

    - Slightly longer messages are more charming for what they reveal about the social dimensions of writing in 12th-century Scandinavia. "Ingebjorg loved me when I was in Stavanger," boasts one. Another reads, "I'd like to get to the pub more often."

- Since these early finds at Bergen, archaeologists have made similar discoveries in the medieval foundations of towns elsewhere in Norway, Sweden, and Denmark and in Viking Age settlements in northern Russia, south Jutland, and even Dublin, Ireland. Still earlier Dark Age settlements in the coastal Netherlands also yield wooden rune sticks.

    o   The medium of wood was ideal for short messages and the simple identification of goods. Carving in wood was simple, cheap, and convenient, and once the message was no longer needed, the stick could be shaved again for a reply or simply thrown into the fire as kindling.

    o   In contrast, contemporary Romans got their medium for writing by flaying a sheep or cow for its skin, then preparing, stretching, and cutting the skin before sewing the pieces into a scroll or a book.

    o   The limitations of runes cut in wood, of course, were message length and storage. This may be the reason that the Roman alphabet and its attendant technologies eventually beat out runes in 7th-century Germany, 11th-century England, and Early Modern Scandinavia.

Properties of Early Runes

- At least half of the early fuþark runes can be seen to come from Roman letters; *F, A, R, C, H, N, I, S, T, B, M,* and *O* are all fairly straightforward derivations. Allowing for varying degrees of rotation, the characters for *U, E,* and *L* might also be added. At least five other runes seem to involve the invention of new signs for sounds that didn't exist in Latin (or the Roman alphabet): [Θ], [g], [w], [ŋ], and [z/r]. This really leaves only the origins of four signs unaccounted for: *J, Ï, P,* and *D.*

- Although the shape and value of the runes seem to reasonably derive from the Roman alphabet, rune names and order clearly deviate from Roman practice. This is somewhat surprising given the stability of the names of the alphabet letters from Phoenician through to the early Roman alphabet and given that the order of the letters has also been maintained through numerous borrowings. It seems that runes were given Germanic names that, wherever possible, begin with the sound whose value they carried.

- The rune names were clearly important to the idea of the runic alphabet. We know this because even though the runes signal consonants and vowels used to spell words, they can also be used as *logograms* ("word signs"), conveying their rune names as words in themselves. Examples of this use can be found in inscribed jewelry, the *Beowulf* manuscript, and the Lindisfarne Gospels.

- So close was the association between rune name and rune that sound changes in the Germanic languages affected the rune value through the rune name. Thus, when Anglo-Frisian, an early ancestor of English, underwent sound changes that changed the word *ansuz* ("god") to *aas* and then *os*, the fourth rune, *ansuz*, itself became *os*, and the rune began to represent the letter *O*!

Uses of Runes
- Our earliest attested use of runes is to write personal names. As mentioned in Lecture 2, this is a common pattern, and proper names may have provided the motivation for phonetic writing in the first place. Apart from the utility of being able to write one's name, the Roman-derived script was also prestigious, perhaps providing an additional motivation for borrowing.

- Despite the practical motivations for borrowing and the mundane personal objects with owners' names that dominate the first few hundred years of runic writing, the eventual outcome was inspiring: 1,500 years of writing and the earliest written records of the Germanic languages.

- Runes were used for many centuries by different peoples to represent different languages; as a result, they changed significantly over time. Variations across different times and regions allow runic specialists to identify fakes easily.

- The fact that so many objects record the names of their makers in runes suggests that literacy may have been limited to a small group of rune masters. This fits with what little we know of early Germanic cultures from Roman historical sources, which depict them as largely oral. Whatever specific purposes writing served, they seem to have been different from contemporary Latin purposes.

- There is a popular notion that early Germanic runes were adopted as magical devices, but this idea is not supported by the evidence. It's true that some inscriptions seem to record magical spells, but this is true of most scripts, including our own.

Eventually, runes would decorate Viking Age runestones, monuments raised in memory of the deceased or erected by the living to commemorate successful conquests.

- It's often argued that the demise of the runes was inevitable with the Roman Catholic Church stamping out pagan customs, but church officials did not go out of their way to restrict the use of runes.

  ○ Rather, it seems that runes entered into competition with and were defeated by their own source script: the Roman alphabet. Given the prestige lent to it by the church, the Roman alphabet began to be adopted for the everyday purposes that runes had once served, and the new alphabet proved equally practical and adaptable.

  ○ Nonetheless, runes continued to survive in England and Scandinavia alongside Christianity and the Roman alphabet. In England, it wasn't until the Norman Conquest of A.D. 1066 that runes succumbed to the Roman alphabet. In Scandinavian countries, the runes persisted through the High Middle Ages and even into Early Modern times. Only then did they slowly become an antiquarian curiosity and pass out of regular use.

Important Terms

Germanic: A subgroup of the Indo-European family of languages that includes German, Dutch, Frisian, Swedish, Icelandic, and English, among others.

logogram (or **logograph**, **lexical sign**): Literally a "word sign," a logogram denotes a specific word and its meaning in an underlying language.

rune (also **runic**): The alphabet adopted by Germanic peoples in the 2nd century A.D. The early and continental variants are known as the *fuþark* (after the first six signs), whereas the later Anglo-Saxon derivation is known as the *fuþorc* (as the result of sound change in the fourth sign).

Suggested Reading

Antonsen, "The Runes: The Earliest Germanic Writing System."

Bowman, *Life and Letters on the Roman Frontier*.

Dahm, "Roman Frontier Signalling and the Order of the *Fuþark*."

Elliott, *Runes: An Introduction*.

Moltke, *Runes and Their Origin*.

Page, *Runes*.

———, *Runes and Runic Inscriptions*.

———, *An Introduction to English Runes*.

Stephens, *Handbook of the Old-Northern Runic Monuments of Scandinavia and England*.

Williams, "The Origin of the Runes."

———, "Reasons for Runes."

1. Did the introduction of Christianity to northwestern Europe spell the end of Germanic runes? Why or why not?

2. Were you surprised to discover that runes were just an ordinary writing system rather than a magical script? Why do you suppose the mystical interpretation of runes remains so popular?

Chinese—A Logosyllabic Script
Lecture 5

In the last couple of lectures, we've looked at numerous alphabets, all of which are phonetic writing systems. Chinese, in contrast, is a logosyllabic writing system. It's an entirely different and much more complex way of representing language, and it seems strange and challenging to those of us who are accustomed to alphabets. Chinese writing is the oldest script in continuous use and one of the most complex writing systems ever devised, with thousands of signs. A study of this rich system has much to teach us about the underlying similarities of writing in all times and places and corrects longstanding notions about the supposed superiority of Western alphabets.

The "Chinese Language"

- The Chinese script is known as *Hànzì*, a Mandarin Chinese term that means, essentially, "Chinese characters." The Han are a dominant Chinese ethnic group, and Han was the name of a dynasty that ruled China from the 3rd century B.C. to the 3rd century A.D. Chinese writing is also the source of several other Asian scripts, including those of Japan, Korea, and Vietnam.

- What we might think of as the "Chinese language" is, in fact, eight mutually unintelligible regional languages, each of which contains numerous *dialects*. These eight regional languages, which include Cantonese and Mandarin, are all members of the *Sino-Tibetan* language family. For most of its history, China's capital has been in the Mandarin-speaking region; thus, Mandarin has become the national common tongue.
  - Today, about 70 percent of modern Chinese people, regardless of their first language, have learned to speak and read Mandarin.

  - In contrast, only 5 percent of Chinese people speak Cantonese as their first language.

- It's sometimes said that speakers of Mandarin or Cantonese, who can't understand one another if communicating in person, can nonetheless communicate in writing. People believe that Chinese writing bridges languages. Some have even extended this idea to include Japanese, Korean, and Vietnamese speakers, because these languages have borrowed Chinese *characters* for their own scripts.
  - In fact, speakers of Cantonese and other Chinese languages cannot understand modern written Chinese without learning Mandarin.

  - Remember our basic definition of a writing system: Writing systems transcribe the sounds of a language. And the sounds of Mandarin, not to mention its grammar and vocabulary, are different enough from other Chinese languages that one can't understand the written language without understanding the spoken one.

Earliest Chinese Script
- Chinese writing has been in continuous use for almost 3,400 years. Linguists divide the evolution of Chinese script into four major stages: The Great Seal script was used by the Zhou dynasty (c. 1028–221 B.C.); the Small Seal script, by the Qin dynasty (c. 221–206 B.C.); and the Regular script, by the Han dynasty (206 B.C.–A.D. 220). The aptly named Simplified script was introduced by the Communist Party in the 1950s.

- The earliest known Chinese writing is found on objects called Shang oracle bones, dating from about 1400 to 1200 B.C. Diviners used these objects to answer questions about the future and to determine auspicious days for all kinds of endeavors. Unfortunately, the early examples of Chinese writing on these bones are difficult to interpret today. Some of the characters are undoubtedly pictographic in origin, but others are indecipherable.

- Of the 4,500 or so Shang signs known, only 25 percent have been convincingly associated with later Chinese characters. The others have simply disappeared during the past 3,000 years, even as thousands of new signs were being invented. By the time of the Han dynasty, there were about 10,000 characters. By the 12th century, there were 25,000, and by the 18th century, almost 50,000. Today, a core set of about 2,400 characters is enough to read the average Chinese newspaper, magazine article, or novel.

- ○ A Shang sign that is still in use today, although in a different form, is the **ma** sign. It began as a recognizable portrait of a horse, but it was simplified, stylized, and even conventionalized over time.

- ○ The symbol can still be used to write *horse*, but it is most frequently used as a phonetic sign, helping to spell other words that are unrelated to horses.

Chinese Character Types

- • Like signs in other complex writing systems, Chinese characters are of several different types, with somewhat different origins and uses. Conventionally, these are divided into five groups, and the **ma** sign is an example of the first group, the logograms. The pictorial origins of such signs are clear, particularly in their earliest stages, though all of them experience stylization and simplification over time.

- • The second group of Chinese signs comprises ***representational signs***. Not strictly pictographs, these signs instead represent their referents in clever ways. Good examples are the signs for the numbers 1, 2, and 3, represented by groupings of one, two, or three strokes.

- • The third group of signs includes ***relational units***, the combination of two preexisting signs to convey a third concept. A popular example is the combination of the logograms for *sun* and *moon* to convey the general idea of "brightness."

- • The fourth group consists of ***rebus*** signs. In Chinese, these are pictographic signs that convey sound rather than meaning.

- • The fifth and most important type of Chinese character is called ***phonetic-semantic***, and it combines two different signs. The first is a **semantic sign** indicating part of the meaning of a word. The second is a phonetic sign partly indicating its pronunciation. These characters are important because Chinese has many homophones.

○ Part of the reason for this is that Chinese is a tonal language; Chinese **tone** comes from words losing their final consonants over time.

○ Depending on the specific consonant that was lost, the tonal quality may be rising, falling, or both in the space of one vowel. The reason the tones are retained instead of themselves being lost is because they're useful. Tones in Chinese help to differentiate between words that would otherwise be exact homophones.

○ The fifth group of Chinese sign types, phonetic-semantic, doesn't capture the actual tones of the Mandarin language, but it guides knowledgeable readers with subtle clues about the intended message.

○ As we'll see, many other writing systems behave in exactly the same way, including Egyptian hieroglyphs, Mesopotamian cuneiform, and Mycenaean Linear B. Signs providing phonetic and semantic information work in tandem in all these scripts, reducing ambiguity to a manageable level.

• The semantic signs in Chinese writing are sometimes called taxon signs or radicals. Large numbers of characters can be grouped according to whether they contain the semantic signs for *person*, *hand*, *water*, *wood*, *insect*, and so forth. In fact, that's how most popular dictionaries of Chinese characters are organized.

○ Apart from Chinese dictionaries produced by Western scholars, there's no such thing as an alphabetic ordering or grouping of Chinese words by sound. Instead, the search for a word in a Chinese dictionary begins with the section containing its semantic element, after which the character can be located in a subsection based on the number of strokes in its phonetic element.

- This system has undoubtedly helped to fuel the notion that Chinese characters are composed of meanings and abstract organizational features rather than the sounds of the Mandarin language. In reality, however, the shared phonetic signs of most Chinese characters would also make a reasonably good ordering system.

- During the Communist Revolution of the 1950s, the Romanized writing system of **Pinyin** was introduced. Pinyin was intended to democratize Chinese literacy, but the Roman alphabet has always met with resistance from the educated classes.
    - Nonetheless, Pinyin's practical benefits can't be overstated. Not only is it far easier to learn than traditional Chinese characters, but it greatly eases the task of entering Chinese text into computers.

    - Many authorities now agree that the future of Chinese literacy is **digraphia** (the use of two scripts by the same community). That is, Chinese characters would not be replaced by the Roman alphabet but, rather, supplemented by it, leading to a populace conversant in both systems.

- The complicated Chinese sign types didn't appear all at once. In the Shang oracle bone inscriptions, solitary signs were the rule, rather than the combined characters that are most common today. Those signs included pictographic, representational, and rebus signs. Modern Chinese script, in contrast, is characterized by combined characters, especially the phonetic-semantic combinations of sound signs and semantic signs.

Contents of Early Chinese Writing

- In a recent article in the journal *Antiquity*, several scholars noted that the Shang oracle bones appear in a markedly ceremonial context and argued that early divination practices provided the motivation for Chinese writing. In a similar way, the earliest attested writing systems of Mesopotamia and Crete are often argued to have developed from the needs of early bureaucrats to maintain detailed records of taxation and tribute.

- Such arguments tend to confuse the first evidence of writing in a region with its actual origin, yet we all know that archaeological evidence, like fossil evidence of earlier stages of biological organisms, suffers from problems of preservation and sampling. Simply put, the fact that a certain sample is the oldest writing we have doesn't mean it's the oldest writing there was. This is true of any object or entity, but it's particularly true of writing because of its remarkable adaptability.

Given the longstanding importance of brush calligraphy in Chinese writing, it's not difficult to imagine the flowing shapes of certain early signs as having originated as ink on paper.

- In the specific case of Chinese writing, it also seems highly unlikely that the oracle bones reflect the first use of the system. For one thing, the form of these early Chinese signs seems particularly ill-suited to carving. Rather, they look like a fairly clear transplant from a painterly medium. It's also true that more than 1,000 of the earliest Chinese signs can be traced to modern descendants, and these cover a much wider semantic territory than would have been needed for divination alone.

- Finally, as we noted in Lecture 2, it's not really the first evidence of writing in any region that needs explanation. Rather, it is phoneticism that cries out for an explanation as the single most important shared structural feature of all writing systems. Neither the ceremonial nor the bureaucratic hypothesis explains the invention of phonetic signs per se. As we've seen, the most logical explanation is that writing was developed precisely to transcribe sounds.

Important Terms

character: A complex sign in Chinese writing, most often composed of a phonetic sign and a semantic sign, but other combinations are also known.

dialect: A variant form of a language, usually defined by region, class, or socioeconomic group and distinguished from other variants by pronunciation, vocabulary, and grammar.

digraphia: Refers to a situation in which two different scripts are used by the same community, usually for different purposes. Modeled on the linguistic term *diglossia*, referring to the different sociopolitical functions of two languages in a single community.

Hànzì (also **Hanzi**): Literally, "Han sign"; the Mandarin term for Chinese characters.

phonetic-semantic sign: Refers to the most common kind of Chinese character, which combines a semantic sign indicating the semantic class of a word with a phonetic sign indicating its pronunciation (minus tone).

Pinyin: The standard system of Romanized spelling for transliterating Chinese writing; from Mandarin 拼音, *pīn-yīn*, literally "spell-sound."

rebus: A principle of logophonetic scripts whereby a logogram is used for its phonetic value to signal a homophonous word (e.g., Mayan **BAAH**, "gopher," used to write *baah*, "head").

relational unit (or **relational sign**): A type of logogram in which two preexisting signs are combined to convey a third concept, as when the Chinese logogram 日, **rì** ("sun"), and 月, **yuè** ("moon"), combine to form 明, **míng** ("bright").

representational sign (also **iconic sign**): A type of logogram in which the form or orientation of the sign visually signals the word referred to, such as the Chinese signs for the numbers — 1, ⚏ 2, and ☰ 3.

semantic sign (also **determinative**, **taxon**, or **radical**): A sign without a phonetic value of its own, but which signals the semantic class to which an associated logogram or group of phonetic signs belongs. What Linear B scholars traditionally call an ideogram is, thus, a semantic sign.

Sino-Tibetan: A language family that includes Chinese, Tibetan, and many other languages of southern and southeast Asia. Tonal contrasts are a common feature of these languages.

tone: Refers to a phonemic pitch carried by vowels, as in Chinese and other Sino-Tibetan languages. Tone usually results from compensation for the loss of earlier consonants.

Suggested Reading

DeFrancis, *The Chinese Language.*

———, *Visible Speech.*

———, "The Ideographic Myth."

Gelb, *A Study of Writing.*

Logan, *The Alphabet Effect.*

Moore, *Chinese.*

Postgate, Tao Wang, and Wilkinson, "The Evidence for Early Writing."

Sampson, *Writing Systems.*

Steinke, "Script Change in Bronze Age China."

Unger, *Ideogram.*

1. Why is it important that we reconsider the existence of ideographic scripts?

2. Why do you think the Chinese never developed a way to mark tone in their writing system, especially given that this would have saved them the effort of having to memorize thousands of different semantic signs?

Japanese—The World's Most Complex Script
Lecture 6

W ith its lengthy traditions, artistic sophistication, and military might, Chinese civilization dramatically influenced all that came into contact with it. Just as Western civilization looks to Greece and Rome for the origins of its cultural traditions, so, too, do Korea, Japan, and Vietnam look to China. Although the Koreans and Vietnamese have now largely replaced Chinese characters with new alphabets, the Japanese still retain their borrowed script, and the story of the adaptation and alteration of this writing system over the past 15 centuries is both fascinating and instructive. As we'll see, Japanese writing is the most complicated writing system ever devised, yet it's used on a daily basis by more than 100 million people.

Development of Japanese Writing

- Chinese characters first came to Japan in the 1st century A.D., in the form of Chinese inscriptions on official correspondence and on imported luxury items. Chinese coins bearing inscriptions have been found from the same period at numerous archaeological sites in Japan. Prior to contact with China, Japan had no writing of its own.

- Initially, the Japanese must have valued the prestigious appearance of Chinese signs, coming as they did from an ancient and complex agricultural civilization from which so much else was being borrowed. Or perhaps it was only an accident that desired art objects and coins came with artists' signatures and other Chinese signs affixed. Regardless of the precise context of this borrowing, it was about 2,000 years ago that writing arrived in Japan.

- An early-8th-century document chronicles the histories of the first emperors of Japan. Called the *Kojiki*, or "Record of Ancient Matters," it notes that a Korean scholar named Wani came to Japan in the 5th century, bringing knowledge of Chinese writing.

- In the wake of Wani's instruction, the earliest surviving Japanese documents are official correspondence dating to the late 6th and early 7th centuries.
  - Intriguingly, these documents seem to have been written and read only in Chinese. As in Korea and Vietnam, the first official writing in Japan recorded the Chinese language written in Chinese characters (albeit with some Korean innovations).

  - The idea that a writing system and language belong together is a common one. The Roman alphabet initially traveled as a medium for the writing of Latin, and it sometimes took centuries for borrowers to begin using it to record their own vernacular languages.

- Relatively speaking, it didn't take long for the Japanese to begin adapting Chinese writing. The process began in the late 5th century A.D. and immediately had to contend with pronounced differences between Chinese and Japanese.
  - Chinese is what linguists call an *isolating language*, which means that it has many invariable words. This helps to explain the structure of Chinese writing, in which each character roughly stands for one of these words, even though most characters are composed of phonetic and semantic elements.

  - The structure of the Japanese language is quite different, more reminiscent of Indo-European languages, with rich derivations and inflexions. This important difference has profound implications for the way Chinese signs had to be adapted to record the Japanese language.

The *Kanji*
- When the Japanese first began to adapt the Chinese script, they had already borrowed thousands of Chinese words and had been exposed to Chinese writing for centuries. For these reasons, coupled with the lack of any other role model, it was only logical to write the borrowed vocabulary with the signs already used to write them in China and that the Japanese had already practiced.

- Although the Japanese *kanji* are essentially just Chinese Hànzì drafted into service to write Japanese, remember that this borrowing took place 1,500 years ago. There are now numerous differences between these two scripts.

- As we've already seen, the Hànzì are written in Mandarin Chinese, and the characters usually have one invariant pronunciation in that language. But the *kanji* have multiple readings.
  - The *on* reading is the modern Japanese approximation of the Chinese pronunciation of the character at the time it was borrowed. Because Japanese continued to borrow Chinese vocabulary over centuries, and because some *kanji* were borrowed from different regions of China (or even from Korea), there are sometimes several historical and regional Chinese readings for a single sign.

  - In contrast, the *kun* reading of a *kanji* is based on the pronunciation of a native Japanese word that closely approximated the meaning of the Chinese character at the time it was borrowed. As with the Chinese readings, there can be multiple Japanese readings for the same *kanji*, and some *kanji* have no Japanese readings at all, as when the borrowed concept had no exact equivalent in Japanese, such as place names and other proper nouns.

- Chinese and Japanese also differ because hundreds of new *kanji* characters have been created in Japan during the past 1,500 years, and many older *kanji* characters have been given new meanings. These additions and alterations represent further differences between the original Hànzì and derived *kanji*.

- In post–World War II Japan, there were several attempts to simplify the *kanji*, with rather mixed results. As noted in the last lecture, postrevolutionary China of the 1950s also saw several attempts at Hànzì simplification, again with mixed results. Because the two attempts at simplification were uncoordinated, the only unambiguous result has been that many originally identical Hànzì and *kanji* characters now have different shapes, meanings, and phonetic values in the two systems.

The *Kana*

- The late-5th-century ***man'yogana*** system began as a mode of using Hànzì for their sound values to write Japanese. There was a great deal of early variation in this usage, but over time, scribes began to settle on specific signs, even simplifying them and creating a visual distinction between word-based *kanji* and sound-based ***kana***.

Japanese writing is the most complex writing system ever devised, yet Japan has one of the highest literacy rates in the modern world.

© Hemera/Thinkstock.

- Phonetic scripts, such as the *kana*, are what linguists call syllabaries: signs standing for whole syllables composed of a vowel or a consonant-vowel combination. In Japanese, the *kana* have 48 characters representing the various syllables of the Japanese language. There are also several ***diacritics*** that indicate variable pronunciations of the signs to which they are attached.

- Two distinct sets of *kana* evolved over time: a plain variant used for literary and official documents and a ***cursive*** variant mostly used for correspondence.
  - The characteristically straight strokes, angular corners, and somewhat simpler shapes of the official script developed into the ***katakana***.

○ The characteristically rounded cursive *kana* **syllabary** developed into the modern *hiragana* script.

• The invention of the *kana* scripts had an additional useful outcome. Traditionally, Chinese was written downward in columns and from right to left. The early system also lacked punctuation and mandated the regular spacing of characters and their placement in predictable blocks of consistent shape.

○ Interpreting these monolithic blocks of text represented no great difficulty for the readers of an isolating language, such as Chinese, but it presented immeasurable difficulties for the reader of an *inflectional language*, such as Japanese.

○ Probably for this reason, the alternation of now visually distinct *kanji* and *kana* in the Japanese writing system helps to produce minimal word separations for the reader.

Modern Usage of the *Kanji* and *Kana*

• The *kanji*, in their various readings, are used to write all of the essential roots of the Japanese language: proper and common nouns, adjectives, and verbs.

• The *hiragana* are used to write inflectional endings on verbs and adjectives, particles, and miscellaneous words that either have no *kanji* or whose *kanji* are considered too obscure to read. *Hiragana* also provide useful clues for reading *kanji*.

• The *katakana* are used for onomatopoeia, interjections, and emphasis; for words and names from foreign languages (not including Chinese); and occasionally for indicating the pronunciation of obscure or novel *kanji*.

Maintaining an Intricate System

• Given the complexity we find in Japanese script, it's not surprising that Korea and Vietnam have rejected their earlier Chinese-derived scripts in favor of alphabets. The forces of conservatism, nationalism, and practicality tend to explain why Japan has not done likewise.

- All writing systems tend to be conservative. This has a practical component because earlier records would all need to be rewritten should a writing system be abandoned or significantly transformed.

- Consider, too, the prestige of this ancient script, unique compared to anything in the West, and the long literary tradition in both Japan and China, stretching back 1,500 and 3,400 years, respectively. To give up their distinctive writing, however beneficial, would be to lose their cultural distinction from the West.

- Finally, recall the large influx of Chinese loanwords and Sino-Japanese coinages in Japanese. If homophones are common in Chinese compared with English, then they truly abound in Japanese. Moreover, in borrowing many Chinese words, Japanese leveled crucial tonal and consonantal distinctions, turning numerous Chinese sound-alikes into precise homophones and producing a truly ambiguous vocabulary.

- For these reasons, a phonetic script alone is not adequate to the task of writing the Japanese language. Even the native *katakana*, which can function as a kind of phonetic alphabet, wouldn't be up to the challenge. Rather, a ***logographic script***, supplemented by sound signs to address derivations and inflections, more usefully disambiguates the thousands of Japanese homophones.

Japanese Civilization
- The Japanese script not only reflects cultural traditions very different from those of the West, but it has also, in turn, imparted something to them. Japanese society was long characterized by an aristocratic leisure class whose only occupation was the production of cultural norms for civilized living. More concerned with baroque refinement than practicality, this class left an indelible imprint on Japanese writing.

- During the Heian period, between A.D. 794 and 1185, Buddhist, Taoist, and other Chinese influences were at their height in Japan. This period is widely considered the peak of the Japanese imperial court, noted for its art, poetry, and literature.

  o What's less commonly known is that the prestigious *kanji* were still the plaything of educated Japanese males during this period. Only the relatively lowly *hiragana* were available to women. As a result, some of the most important works of Heian literature were produced by women and written in *hiragana*, including *The Tale of Genji*.

  o The irony is twofold. Not only was this masterpiece produced in a script that was underappreciated at the time, but we can actually still read *Genji* in the Japanese of that era, whereas other works produced in *kanji* are more semantic than phonetic, and scholars are not always sure how they would have been pronounced 1,000 years ago.

- But the Japanese *kanji* are no longer the plaything of an otherwise idle elite, nor are the *hiragana* relegated to secondary status. Rather, these and other writing systems are welded into a complex whole used by the entire literate population of Japan—one of the largest in the modern world.

Important Terms

cursive: Generally speaking, *cursive* refers to writing with joined characters, as in the longhand once taught in grade school. But some scripts designed for rapid writing with ink on paper are also known as *cursive*, such as Egyptian demotic, Japanese *hiragana*, and Aramaic abjad.

diacritic: A sign that does not have a phonetic value of its own but signals a change in value of signs with which it is associated. In French, when the letter *c* appears with a cedilla (ç), it is no longer pronounced [k] but, rather, [s], as in the word *façade*.

hiragana: Japanese syllabary used to write inflectional endings on verbs and adjectives (behaving as phonetic complements) and to write grammatical particles and miscellaneous words that have no *kanji* or whose *kanji* are obscure.

inflectional language (or **synthetic language**): A language in which the grammatical relationships between words in a sentence are determined by inflections (such as case endings). Some languages, such as Nahuatl, are what might be called hyperinflectional, building lengthy words out of the agglutination of many distinct morphemes.

isolating language (or **analytic language**): A language in which the grammatical relationships between words in a sentence are determined by word order rather than case endings or similar grammatical inflections.

kana: Either of the two Japanese syllabaries (*katakana* and *hiragana*).

katakana: Japanese syllabary used to spell names in foreign languages (not including Chinese) and for onomatopoeia, interjections, and emphasis.

kun (or *kun'yomi*): The value of a *kanji* based on the pronunciation of a native Japanese word that closely approximated its meaning when first introduced. Some *kanji* have multiple *kun* readings; others, none at all.

logographic script: A writing system composed entirely of logograms. A conceptual category only because there are no known writing systems without phonetic signs.

man'yogana: The early Chinese characters used in 5th-century Japan for their sound values alone, eventually giving rise to the two *kana* syllabaries.

on (or *on'yomi*): The value of a *kanji* based on the Japanese pronunciation of its Chinese reading when first introduced. Some *kanji* have multiple *on* readings, whereas those invented more recently in Japan usually have none.

syllabary: A writing system composed, in whole or in part, of syllabic signs. The Inuktitut syllabary is composed entirely of syllabic signs, but most syllabaries are part of more complex scripts. Examples of these include Linear B (with its many semantic signs), Old Persian (with a few logograms), Mayan (with hundreds of logograms), and Japanese (with two syllabaries and thousands of logograms).

Suggested Reading

Goody and Watt, "The Consequences of Literacy."

Lurie, "The Development of Writing in Japan."

McLuhan, *The Gutenberg Galaxy.*

Miller, *The Japanese Language.*

Miyake, *Old Japanese.*

Sampson, *Writing Systems.*

Sansom, *Japan: A Short Cultural History.*

Seeley, *A History of Writing in Japan.*

Questions to Consider

1. Why is Japanese writing so complex? In your answer, try to tease apart the historical reasons for the script's complexity (that is, its origins and development over time) from the social, political, and economic reasons for its continued use.

2. What does the high Japanese literacy rate tell us about the connection between complexity of a script and literacy? How does (or should) this influence policies for improving literacy worldwide?

What Is Decipherment?
Lecture 7

In the last few lectures, we've defined writing, traced the origins of the earliest scripts, and charted the development of the alphabet and Chinese characters, the two most common writing systems still in use today. Before we dive deeper in our exploration, looking at the structure and contents of early scripts and their reflection of the sociopolitical organization of the early civilizations that used them, we need to discuss archaeological decipherment. In particular, we need to learn something about the theory and methodology of decipherment, as well as the evidence it considers. In this lecture, we'll ask: How do we know what we think we know about ancient writing systems? And how certain are we in that knowledge?

Archaeological Decipherment
- One common definition of the verb *decipher* is "to convert a text written in *code* into ordinary language." This definition assumes that *decipherment* involves an intentionally hidden or secret message. But specialists in the decipherment of ancient writing systems do not use the word *decipher* in this way, and there's no reason to believe that early Egyptian, Mesopotamian, or Chinese scribes were engaged in the secret encoding of their languages.

- A second definition, "to interpret hieroglyphics or obscure inscriptions," is also a bit misleading. Decipherment is much broader as a practice than is suggested by the narrow term *hieroglyphics*.
  - This definition seems to indicate that only Egyptologists or those interested in strange, exotic scripts practice decipherment. In fact, archaeological decipherment concerns itself with all writing systems everywhere, including even the earlier attested stages of modern writing systems, such as the alphabet and Chinese.

  - The word *interpret* in this definition is also a bad choice because it carries a strong sense of subjectivity. Archaeological decipherment is a scientific discipline that marshals evidence to establish the structure and meaning of ancient writing. There aren't multiple interpretations of Egyptian hieroglyphs, though there can certainly be disagreements between scholars when the evidence for one theory or another isn't conclusive.

- As a result of the accomplishments of early scholars in deciphering Egyptian hieroglyphics, cuneiform, and Linear B, the term *decipher* is now also loosely applied to anything especially difficult or obscure that eventually yields to understanding, such as the human genome.

- Just like the definitions for *writing* that we looked at in our first lecture, those commonly used for *decipher* bear only a superficial resemblance to what specialists in decipherment mean when they use the term. In fact, the definition of *decipher* depends on what is meant by *writing*; the terms are linked.
  - Those scholars who favor a broad definition of *writing* as "graphic communication" are fairly well served by some of the popular definitions of decipherment, especially "uncovering the meaning of something obscure or difficult."

  - But if by *writing* we mean only "visible speech"—a system of graphic marks that convey language through the use of phonetic signs—then *decipherment* must be defined technically.

- For our purposes, decipherment is nothing less than a complete account of sign use in a writing system, including details of sign types, orthography, and abbreviational conventions.
  - Note that this definition focuses only on the structural principles of writing. To decipher any writing system, such as ancient Egyptian hieroglyphs, we need to determine first and foremost what kinds of signs it has and then look at how those signs combine to represent the Egyptian language. No interpretation is needed.

  - Note also the word *complete* in our definition, in this case meaning "complete in intention." Decipherment aims for a thorough understanding of the relationship between script and language. In real-world practice, a complete decipherment of many ancient scripts is probably impossible to achieve.

- Decipherment is a longitudinal process, not an isolated event. Not a year goes by without some new discovery shedding light on the value of a previously undeciphered sign or a new word, grammatical construction, or spelling rule in ancient scripts.

- Decipherment has its own place in the history of ideas; it's a development and practice that's unique to the modern world.
    - Only in the wake of the Renaissance and the Enlightenment was there a sufficiently rational, empirical background in place that allowed the diligent comparison of complex phenomena to begin to yield testable hypotheses. For the first time, scholars could trace the origins and development of related entities, testing their predictions against new discoveries and experiments.

    - It's no accident that Darwin's discovery of natural selection and biological evolution, *Grimm's law* of sound changes in the Germanic family of languages, and Jean-François Champollion's decipherment of Egyptian hieroglyphic writing all took place within a few decades of each other in the early 19th century. Those were great and momentous decades, during which the foundations of most of the sciences were laid.

Epistemology of Decipherment
- The word *epistemology* refers to a "theory of knowledge," especially with regard to its methods, validity, and scope. Epistemology is the investigation of what distinguishes justified belief from mere opinion, received tradition, or authority.

- Historical sciences, such as biology, linguistics, and decipherment, consider as much evidence as possible, comparing large numbers of different organisms, languages, and texts. General laws are inductively inferred from the evidence, and those laws are then tested deductively on new evidence as it emerges. If new evidence doesn't meet the expectations of the general law, then the law is modified to take account of the exceptions.

- This process, too, never ceases. As a result, a scientific theory or general law becomes more robust over time, in that it is repeatedly challenged by evidence and improved to take account of those challenges. This is what defines the scientific method: Nothing is taken as truth based on tradition alone but on the constant accumulation of evidence and testing of hypotheses.

- The focus of decipherment is always on the structural principles of writing. As long as our methods are valid, the evidence is sufficient to the task, and our willingness to discard untenable ideas is unwavering, we can assume that we're increasingly able to read what ancient scribes intended.
  - Note that this objective experiment in the recovery of ancient writing and the language it records isn't the same thing as the interpretation of a text's meaning. Here, we enter into an all-too-human realm where subjectivity of various kinds becomes inescapable. Too often, we don't even recognize that we're being subjective, so engrained are the habits and preoccupations of our own culture.

  - As soon as the decipherer's task is done, the comforting certainty of phonetic signs, logographs, and spelling rules gives way to a text written in a foreign language, with all the attendant perils of translation, not to mention exaggeration, bias, propaganda, and even the effects of simple human forgetfulness.

  - Fortunately, historians have developed a successful approach to written records called *historiography*. By comparing and contrasting different independent accounts of past events, they can weigh those accounts and weed out error, whether intentional or otherwise.

Code Breaking versus Decipherment

- Code breakers (sometimes called cryptanalysts or cryptographers) apply their trade to messages intentionally enciphered to hide their plain meaning. Decipherers (sometimes called *epigraphers* or epigraphists) work to understand writing systems that were never intended to be secret, but whose conventions have been lost over time.

- Another important difference between code breaking and decipherment is that cryptographers work with fewer variables than epigraphers.
  - Cryptographers already know a great deal about the origins of the encoded messages they confront, including the identity of the sender and the language of the actual message hidden in the code.

  - Epigraphers, in contrast, often work in the dark. Many ancient texts can't be associated with a known culture or language; either or both may need to be reconstructed or may have been lost entirely. Further, epigraphers have the task of learning about ancient languages from the very texts they're trying to decipher, which means that they often can't rely on the favorite tricks of the cryptanalyst, such as *frequency analysis*.

- Despite the differences between code breaking and decipherment, however, there are some similarities. When the conditions are right, an epigrapher may be able to guess at the underlying language of an ancient inscription, and provided the evidence exists to reconstruct some of that language independently, its patterns and grammar can be applied as an aid to decipherment.

History of Cryptography

- Two thousand years ago, Julius Caesar designed his own substitution code for use during his military campaigns in Gaul, Germania, and Britain. Perhaps surprisingly, the Caesar cipher continued to be used in military engagements even as late as World War I. The Caesar cipher is vulnerable to so-called brute force attacks, in which an intercepted code is subjected to endless letter shifts until the gibberish turns into language. As a result, much more subtle and complex codes emerged between the two world wars.

- Perhaps the most famous wartime code was the complex and frequently changing substitution cipher made possible by the German Wehrmacht's Enigma machine. This device incorporated a set of rotors or wheels, a lampboard, a keyboard, and a hidden plugboard.

The Enigma machine required a list of daily key settings, which were set out in code books; despite the Germans' precautions, the Allies managed to capture several of the code books and the machines themselves.

  - The operator used the rotors to set an encryption key (a protocol that specified letter shifts and sequences) and simply typed the plaintext onto the keyboard while noting and transcribing the ciphered text lighting up the lampboard. An encrypted message could be read by reversing the process. The key to the system's success was the frequently changing encryption key.

  - Code breakers in Britain worked to uncover the daily settings of the Enigma machines using a device called a Bombe that replicated Enigma's actions.

- The Allies used the Navajo language as a code during the war in the Pacific. This language was completely unknown to the Japanese because it was unwritten and had never been studied by Japanese linguists. An additional layer of code was used on top of the Navajo language to enable the inclusion of such terms as *aircraft carrier*, *plane*, and so on.

• As we said, the variables involved in decipherment are generally much greater than those in code breaking, and sometimes, they can't be resolved. Indeed, decipherment is mostly a process of solving for variables. Where the right conditions exist, epigraphers are able to puzzle out the details of lost scripts and their underlying languages. Where the right conditions are wanting, epigraphers have learned that an attempted decipherment may be little better than a guess.

Important Terms

code: A secret message. Codes are broken by code breakers (also cryptanalysts or cryptographers). Despite some overlap in methodology, code breaking is not decipherment.

decipherment: A complete account of sign use in a writing system, including details of sign types, orthography (i.e., spelling rules), and abbreviational conventions.

epigrapher (also **epigraphist**): Specialist in the study of writing systems.

epistemology: The theory of knowledge, particularly with regard to its methods, validity, and scope. The investigation of what distinguishes justified belief from opinion or tradition.

frequency analysis: Study of the repetition of signs or sign groups in a text in order to draw conclusions based on the known frequencies of letters and words in the language it represents.

Grimm's law: A complex series of sound changes, first described by Jacob Grimm in 1822, that turned Proto-Indo-European *p* into Germanic *f*, among other related changes. Hence, Latin *pater* (which didn't undergo the change) compared to English *father* (which did).

historiography: The comparison and contrast of historical records to resolve biases and contradictions.

Suggested Reading

Coe, *Breaking the Maya Code.*

Friedrich, *Extinct Languages.*

Gordon, *Forgotten Scripts.*

Kahn, *The Codebreakers.*

Pope, *The Story of Decipherment.*

Robinson, *Lost Languages.*

———, *The Story of Writing.*

Questions to Consider

1. How do we know what we think we know about ancient biology, linguistics, and writing systems? What other fields of study value the formation of hypotheses and rigorous testing on new evidence as it becomes available?

2. How are decipherment and code breaking similar, and how they different? Were you surprised to discover that no famous code breakers have ever deciphered an ancient writing system? Why or why not?

The Five Pillars of Decipherment
Lecture 8

In this lecture, we explore what the Mayanist Michael Coe has called the "five pillars of decipherment." At least a few of these pillars have to be in place before any decipherment of an ancient script is even possible, and all of them are necessary if we are to recover a complete picture of an ancient writing system. Understanding the five pillars goes a long way toward explaining why some writing systems were seemingly deciphered so quickly, while others took many years of concerted effort and still others remain completely mysterious.

Understanding the Five Pillars

- In his accessible history of the decipherment of Maya writing, *Breaking the Maya Code*, the Mayanist scholar Michael Coe refers to five "fundamental pillars on which all successful decipherments have rested." These five pillars are script type; corpus; language; cultural context; and *bilingual, biscript,* or *constraint.*

- Script type refers to the idea that epigraphers must know the type of writing system they're dealing with, that is, whether it's an alphabet; a syllabary; or a mixed script combining word signs, semantic signs, and sound signs.

- Corpus refers to the body of texts available for study, that is, the database of known texts in the writing system. This needs to be large and varied enough to allow effective comparisons, and there should be at least a few long texts, ideally with a diversity of genres.

- Language is one of the most important pillars. Put simply, the language recorded by an ancient writing system must be independently known. If the language itself has vanished, then it must be possible to reconstruct it on the basis of recorded dictionaries or grammars or by comparison with languages to which it is related.

- Cultural context refers to the idea that traditions and histories giving place names, royal names, and titles should be independently known. Such information provides an important target for decipherment, which almost always focuses on proper names written phonetically.

- Finally, bilingual, biscript, or constraint refers to certain types of critical clues on which decipherment depends.
  - The most useful of these is a bilingual or multilingual inscription (such as the Rosetta Stone), at least one member of which is in a known writing system recording a known language. This allows the epigrapher to hunt for the proper names of the known inscription in the unknown one, making initial guesses (subject to further testing) as to the values of some of its signs.

  - If there are no bilinguals, the corpus should at least contain some texts closely associated with illustrations (*picture biscripts*) or other similar constraints providing clues to sound values or meanings.

- The five pillars are not only preconditions that make decipherment possible, but they're also measures of the amount that can be learned from any given ancient script. Just as multiple bilinguals with multiple writing systems increase our certainty of the sound values of an ancient script, so, too, does the presence of each additional pillar add substantially to the foundational strength of a decipherment.

- The best-known ancient writing systems are those supported by all five pillars. Writing systems without any of these pillars remain undeciphered. In between is a spectrum of scripts running from the undeciphered through the poorly known to the slightly better known.

Typology of Writing

- The typology of writing is a classification of writing systems according to their various types. As we've seen, all known writing systems are at least minimally alike in that they all contain phonetic signs (that is, signs conveying sound). Yet many writing systems contain other types of signs that combine to give each script its own unique character. The three main types of signs are logograms, *phonograms*, and semantic signs.

- A logogram is a sign representing a given word in a language. This concept is a bit more difficult than it seems.
  - Some words are themselves compounds of two other words (e.g., *snowman*). Words can also be made up of several smaller pieces that linguists call *morphemes*—the smallest indivisible unit of meaning in a language.

  - A crucial point is that logograms are never just signs for ideas or concepts. They are always mapped one-to-one to a word in a given language. The distinction between word and idea is an important one, because it means that logograms convey both sound and meaning. That is, they are indexically linked to the pronunciation of a given word in a language, while also transmitting the meaning of that word.

  - Logograms are present in all of the world's writing systems. Logograms in our alphabet include the Arabic numerals 1 and 4 (when used in rebus fashion for its sound value alone, e.g., *4ever*), the ampersand sign (&), and the "at" sign (@).

  - Logograms in the world's writing systems have varied origins, but what unites them all is that their function in a given writing system is to represent a single word within the language.

- Phonograms, the second major sign type, represent only sound, never meaning.
  - We're naturally most familiar with the mixture of signs for single consonants and vowels that characterizes our own

alphabet. And if we think back to the origins of our alphabet in the Phoenician abjad, we can comprehend a different set of phonetic signs representing only consonants.

o   Apart from signs for single consonants and single vowels, we've also seen phonetic signs in Chinese and Japanese writing that take the form of full pronounceable syllables. These so-called *syllabic signs* cue either pure vowels (such as **i**, **e**, **a**, **o**, **u**) or a consonant followed by a vowel (such as **na**). Other writing systems have still other shapes for their phonetic signs, such as several of the older cuneiform scripts.

o   Because of this variation, phonetic signs can seem like a ragtag assortment. What unites them is their shared function in all these writing systems. As signs conveying sound but not meaning, they can be used additively to spell words. Thus, in Maya writing, the signs **ba-la-ma** spell the word *bahlam*, "jaguar," and in Linear B, the signs **pa-ka-na** spell *phasgana*, "swords."

o   Another shared function of phonetic signs is to provide *phonetic complements* to logograms, giving clues to their reading values or adding derivational or inflectional suffixes. We've seen examples of this intriguing practice in Japanese, where the *hiragana* phonetic signs are used to complement and derive *kanji* logograms.

o   Like logograms, phonetic signs can also originate as pictographs. Recall the origins of our own letters *A* and *B* as early depictions of an ox and a house. And recall the pictorial origins of several phonetic elements in Chinese characters, such as the "horse" sign, **ma**. The phonetic signs of the Egyptian hieroglyphs, Sumerian cuneiform, and Mayan and Aztec writing also derive from pictures of objects and entities.

•   The third major sign type, semantic signs, are sometimes called determinatives, taxon signs, or radicals. Unlike logograms and phonetic signs, semantic signs have no sound value. They also aren't linked to specific words of a language. Instead, they convey concepts or ideas, but they don't do so alone. Rather, semantic signs always appear alongside logograms and phonetic signs to help disambiguate the semantic range (or meaning) of the words being spelled.

- o As we saw in Lecture 5, the most common type of Chinese character is the phonetic-semantic type, which combines a phonetic sign (partially spelling a word, though without indicating the important distinctions of tone) and a semantic sign (helping to disambiguate the many potential homophones of the Chinese language).

- o Egyptian hieroglyphs work the same way and for a similar reason. Because Egyptian scribes did not write vowels, hieroglyphs provide only the consonantal skeletons of words, leaving a great deal of ambiguity for the reader. The semantic signs serve to alleviate this ambiguity, indicating that a particular group of phonetic signs is to be interpreted as a word meaning "skin, mammal, or leather" or "small, bad, or weak."

Sign Counts

- The structure and behavior of these sign types has implications for the number of signs a writing system has. Provided there are enough examples of a writing system (that is, a sufficiently large and well-recorded body of texts), epigraphers can actually derive a more-or-less accurate idea of the type of writing system just by counting the number of visually distinct signs.

- Granted, some signs have multiple values, and it's not always easy to tell apart signs that are truly distinct from signs that merely appear distinct because of different handwriting, regional variations, or change through time. But this unavoidable uncertainty is only significant in writing systems that already have a large number of different signs, which already puts them in one of the categories.

- Michael Coe assembled a useful chart indicating the number of distinct signs in several writing systems, ancient and modern.

- Certain scripts, such as Chinese and Egyptian, have thousands of signs because they contain many logograms, phonograms, and semantic signs.

- Other structurally similar scripts, such as Sumerian and Mayan, have fewer signs, but the number is usually still in the hundreds.

- Syllabaries do not have nearly as many signs as Mayan but still have two to three times as many signs as alphabets, because they combine consonants and vowels into the same sign.

- Such scripts as our alphabet are all consonants and vowels, with only a few logographs and semantic signs; thus, they have a relatively small number of signs overall.

- There's an overlap between alphabets and consonant-only scripts (abjads), which means that we can't be certain from sign counts alone whether scripts with 30 or so signs definitely have vowels or not. Similarly, some alphabets with large numbers of signs can enter the distribution of syllabaries with low numbers of signs; thus, it's also not always possible to distinguish syllabaries and alphabets on sight.

- But the high, middle, and low ends of the distribution remain neatly separate. On the basis of sign count alone, scholars usually know if they're dealing with a mixed *logosyllabic* or *logoconsonantal script*, a syllabary, or an abjad. As we'll see, this is a remarkable boon for decipherment.

- All known writing systems, ancient and modern, fall into one of the types described here, with some complications regarding scripts with low sign counts. By an interesting accident, the two major systems of writing still in use today (the alphabet and Chinese characters) also exemplify two of the major typological categories of writing.

Number of Signs in Ancient and Modern Writing Systems

Writing System	Number of Signs
Mixed scripts (logosyllabic/logophonetic)	
Chinese characters	50,000
Japanese *kanji*	50,000
Egyptian hieroglyphs	2,500
Sumerian cuneiform	600+
Mayan glyphs	500+
Syllabaries	
Linear B (Mycenaean Greek)	87
Cherokee	85
Japanese (*hiragana* only)	42
Old Persian	36
Alphabets	
Russian	36
Old English	31
Modern English	26
Germanic Fuþark	24
Abjads	
Arabic	28
Hebrew	22

List adapted from Coe (1992:43) and Gelb (1952:115).

- To summarize, ***mixed scripts*** all have logographs, phonetic signs, and semantic signs. Syllabaries all have signs representing pronounceable combinations of sounds (that is, syllables), sometimes combined with logographs and semantic signs. Alphabets and abjads all have signs for minimally contrastive speech sounds, occasionally with some logographs and semantic signs.

bilingual: An inscription containing two (or more) distinct languages, whether written in the same or different scripts. In cases where more than two languages are involved, scholars occasionally refer to the inscriptions as trilingual, quadrilingual, multilingual, and so on.

biscript: An inscription containing two (or more) distinct scripts, whether recording the same or different languages. In cases where more than two scripts are involved, scholars occasionally refer to them as triscripts, quadriscripts, multiscripts, and so on.

constraint: Refers to a useful clue in decipherment, such as a picture biscript or two historically related scripts sharing signs of the same form and value.

logoconsonantal script: A writing system composed of logograms and consonantal signs.

logosyllabic script (or **logosyllabary**): A writing system composed of logograms and syllabic signs, such as Mayan and Aztec writing.

mixed script: A general term for a logophonetic script.

morpheme: The smallest indivisible unit of meaning in a language. The English word *tapping* is composed of two morphemes: the verbal root *tap* and the bound morpheme *-ing*, indicating a participle or gerund. (The doubled *p* is an orthographic device cueing the short vowel of *tap* in *tapping*, rather than the historic long vowel of *tape* in *taping*.)

phonetic complement: A phonetic sign used to clarify the reading of an associated logogram, indicating (and at least partially reiterating) its reading. Often, this is done to provide a grammatical inflection to a verb root provided by the logogram, as in Japanese and Mayan.

phonetic sign (or **phonogram**): A sign for an abstract sequence of sound. Phonetic signs do not carry meaning and come in numerous formal varieties, including consonants (C), vowels (V), consonant groups (CC and CCC), consonant-vowel groups (CV), vowel-consonant groups (VC), and even consonant-vowel-consonant groups (CVC). But no script has all of these forms. For instance, Egyptian phonetic signs are only C, CC, and CCC (e.g., **n**, **nb**, and **nfr**) and Maya phonetic signs are only V and CV (e.g., **a** and **ka**).

picture biscript: A close association between text and image (as in a caption), whereby the image provides a helpful constraint on the meaning of the text.

syllabic sign (or **syllabogram**): A phonetic sign representing a pronounceable syllable and, therefore, always including a vowel either alone or preceded and/or followed by a consonant. For example, the Maya signs **a** and **ka** are syllabic signs, as are the Aztec signs **o**, **to**, and **ol**.

Suggested Reading

Coe, *Breaking the Maya Code* (especially chapter 1).

Daniels, "Fundamentals of Grammatology."

Daniels and Bright, eds., *The World's Writing Systems*.

Friedrich, *Extinct Languages*, especially "Principles of the Methodology of the Decipherment of Extinct Scripts and Languages."

Gelb, *A Study of Writing*.

Gordon, *Forgotten Scripts*.

Pope, *The Story of Decipherment*.

Questions to Consider

1. Without reviewing the guidebook or the lecture, what are the five pillars of decipherment? Put them into your own words and explain why each of them is important. Are some more important than others? Which ones, and why?

2. How does knowing the type of a writing system help in decipherment? Do you think decipherment would be possible without knowing this?

Epigraphic Illustration
Lecture 9

In the last lecture, we learned that epigraphers have long exploited the inherent formal variation of writing systems. Simply by counting the number of visually distinct signs, scholars can broadly determine the type of a given writing system. This visual dimension of writing explains why our discussion of script typology has until now been focused on the graphic variation of signs. We've also observed that the visual nature of writing inevitably interacts with the medium on which it's recorded; that is, writing is not itself a medium but relies on other media for its transmission. It's this materiality of writing that concerns us in this lecture. We turn now to the second pillar of decipherment: the corpus, or body of texts available for study.

Requirements for a Corpus

- Scholars can't decipher a writing system without a large body of texts from which to draw examples, deduce patterns, and test hypotheses. Ideally, the texts should be of different types and lengths and represent a variety of different subjects.

- The undeciphered Indus script, used in what is now Pakistan between the 3rd and 2nd millennia B.C., serves as an example here.
  - This writing system is known from thousands of different texts on small soapstone seals (and their impressions in clay), yet all of these texts are short, and all of them probably give only the names and titles of their owners.

  - In this instance, we lack most of the other pillars. Scholars aren't certain about the language or the cultural context of Indus civilization, and there are no bilinguals, biscripts, or other constraints. The sheer monotony of the Indus corpus frustrates decipherment. These short texts with their seemingly relentless focus on names and titles give us few of the patterns and repetitions we need for decipherment.

- Of the five pillars, only the type of script is known. The presence of 500 or so distinct signs strongly suggests that the Indus script is a mixed *logophonetic* writing system. But the nature of its phonetic signs—whether consonantal, alphabetic, or syllabic—also remains unknown, despite decades of intensive work.

- In contrast, deciphered writing systems all have large numbers of inscriptions with at least some topical breadth, and most are also characterized by a broad materiality, appearing on numerous media.
  - Egyptian hieroglyphic writing, for example, was carved on interior and exterior walls, on the sides of *obelisks*, and on wooden boxes. It was inlaid into gold and silver and painted on caskets and fragile *papyrus* scrolls.

  - Each of these contexts conveyed different types of messages, giving every hieroglyphic sign in the Egyptian writing system ample opportunity to show itself in several contexts.

- The fact that scholarship requires a large number of texts of different types presents an unavoidable practical consideration: No one scholar would ever be able to gather together every example of an ancient civilization's writing for private study; indeed, attempting to make such a collection would be ethically irresponsible. Because of this, the need for a broad and representative corpus carries a corollary requirement that texts be both accurately recorded and freely available to scholars.

Recording Inscriptions

- Some of the earliest records of inscriptions were rubbings. This process works by overlaying an inscription with a piece of paper or cloth and then rubbing a piece of charcoal or crayon along the surface, catching details of the carved surface below. Rubbing was a favorite recording method for hundreds of years, but rubbings of larger inscriptions can be difficult to store and keep clean; for this reason, rubbing is no longer common.

- Making large three-dimensional copies of inscriptions—usually plaster casts fashioned from paper and plaster molds—was an important method of recording in the late 19th and early 20th centuries. Usually, the maker would press paper and plaster into an inscription, dry it out, and then carefully peel off the hardened paper to use it as a mold from which to cast a plaster copy. Molds were taken from monumental inscriptions around the world, and the plaster casts made from them are still found in museums.
  - In some cases, early plaster casts are the only accurate three-dimensional records we have of monuments that were afterward eroded, intentionally damaged, or even destroyed.

  - Of course, full-scale replicas of original monuments can be quite large and heavy, and the plaster is often fragile. They are also expensive to transport and store, which is why they've mostly fallen into disfavor.

- Photography was the technology that largely supplanted both rubbings and plaster casts. Early cameras were large format, with large glass-plate negatives almost 10 times the size of later 35mm cameras, thereby providing a wealth of detail.
  - Early photographic records of inscriptions are invaluable to scholars because they reveal the fine incisions that can be difficult to capture in a rubbing and because they document many more inscriptions than anyone would ever be able to make into plaster casts.

  - Storage of large glass-plate negatives is difficult and expensive; thus, these early formats were retired as soon as the technology matured and miniaturized. Film cameras are now being steadily replaced by digital cameras, and the more recent of these are even beginning to approach the quality of the earliest large-format cameras. Digital photography is likely to remain a staple recording technology for the foreseeable future.

- Three-dimensional scanning is the newest technology to come onto the scene. With this approach, several cameras (or scanners) take a detailed, high-resolution topography of an object and render it as a three-dimensional digital model. The model can be stitched together with others, producing elaborate three-dimensional replicas of (potentially) entire temple complexes with walls covered in hieroglyphs.

Line Drawings

- Despite the use of these other technologies, most publications of inscriptions rely on nothing fancier than line drawings. Such drawings are a simple and effective way to reproduce a text for study by epigraphers and have a number of practical and theoretical advantages over other means of recording inscriptions, including their low cost, convenience of storage, and ease of transmission.

- A key advantage of line drawings from the point of view of decipherment is clarity and comprehensiveness. Unlike in a photograph, the visual field in a line drawing can be simplified and clarified. Scratches and gaps can be filled in, and shadows, surface texture, and dust and dirt can all be removed.
  - A single line drawing can incorporate information collected from several perspectives using multiple light sources to maximize the contrast between the background and the text. In some cases, imaging outside of the visible range (such as infrared and ultraviolet) can be used to help reconstruct damaged portions of text.

  - Line drawings are, therefore, composite images of a text that capture much more detail than may be apparent at first glance or with a single shutter click. They represent more than can be seen by the human eye under even the most optimal viewing conditions.

- Line drawings also present a few disadvantages. They don't capture color, they can only approximate the three-dimensional properties of an object, and they are subjective.

o   The first disadvantage follows more from longstanding conventions of publication and needn't be strictly true. Colored drawings and even color photographs now accompany many black-and-white journal articles as online content.

o   The second disadvantage highlights the utility of rubbings, casts, and three-dimensional scans, which will therefore never be wholly replaced by line drawings. Perhaps three-dimensional scans accompanying drawings in published sources as online content will one day become standard in epigraphy, allowing the reader to rotate and view the scanned inscription from multiple directions with multiple lighting sources.

o   The third disadvantage—the inherent subjectivity of line drawings—has historically posed the greatest barrier to decipherment. Early drawings of ancient monuments were made before the establishment of guidelines for the acceptable illustration of archaeological finds. Linked to this was the consideration that accurate recording was seen as secondary to artistic interpretation or inspiration.

•   Despite their disadvantages, line drawings remain an important tool for the decipherer. Epigraphers today work with any and all records of an inscription available to them, particularly if the inscriptions are damaged or unclear. But provided archaeological illustrators have done their jobs properly, this should be necessary only in extreme cases. Ideally, the illustrators themselves have weighed the evidence from the original texts and such rubbings, casts, and photographs as could be found in producing their final illustrations.

Modern Epigraphic Illustration
•   The process of epigraphic illustration today usually begins with field sketches in front of the original monument. If a text is lightly incised, weathered, or otherwise damaged, variable light will often be used to bring the relief into clearer focus. The use of raking light cast perpendicular to the surface of the stone makes raised reliefs

"pop" and tends to wash out scratches and other damage, making intentional lines clearer.

o   The tactile experience of direct contact with the stone is also invaluable. This is the epigrapher's opportunity to verify the difference between an actual carved line and cracks, root scars, pitting, shadows, and other tricks of the light. Photographs are usually taken at the same time, with a number of light sources and from different directions.

o   Final illustrations are traced directly over photographs, often on acetate, vellum, or another semitransparent film, sometimes using a light table. Increasingly, these illustrations are made directly in a digital medium, using a tablet or similar drawing aid and multiple digital layers in a drawing program.

o   Reference is made during the process to field sketches, photographs, casts, three-dimensional scans, and other available materials. The final drawing is then checked wherever possible against the original, at which time further amendments may be necessary.

•   There are two basic aims in this process: to reduce subjectivity as much as possible and to distill the carved monument into its most essential features.

Shading, cross-hatching, blending, and smudging are the enemies of quality epigraphic illustration, which aims for a clean black-and-white image composed of only lines and dots.

Drawings and photographs of ancient inscriptions by Dr. Marc Zender, Tulane University.

- Epigraphic illustration is not an attempt at realism or an opportunity to express oneself artistically. Rather, the archaeological illustrator is engaged in producing a schematic guide to the original monument in which all purposeful details are highlighted.

- All artifacts of the later history of the monument, such as weathering, damage, inexpert repair, and so forth, are presented in as straightforward and nondistracting a manner as possible. Interesting as they are, these are not the epigrapher's main interest or concern, which remains always focused on the intentional aspects of the carving.

- Still, epigraphic illustration remains more art than science, and to pretend otherwise would be to deceive ourselves. And drawing an inscription is more than a passive recording technique. It's an active process of engagement with every detail of an inscription.

Important Terms

logophonetic script: A writing system composed of logograms and phonetic signs (without specifying whether the latter are consonantal, alphabetic, or syllabic).

obelisk: A monumental stone pillar, usually with a square cross-section and a pyramidal apex.

papyrus: A tall, aquatic sedge (*Cyperus papyrus*), native to central Africa and the Nile valley and from which the earliest paper was made. Early Semitic and Greek words for this plant are the sources of the English words *paper*, *bible*, and *bibliography*.

Suggested Reading

Adkins and Adkins, *Archaeological Illustration*.

Banta, Hinsley, and O'Donnell, *From Site to Sight*.

Fane, "Reproducing the Pre-Columbian Past."

Fash, "Cast Aside."

Smiles and Moser, eds., *Envisioning the Past.*

Steiner, *Approaches to Archaeological Illustration.*

Questions to Consider

1. In what ways is it significant that writing is a graphic medium? In what ways is Braille both tactile and graphic?

2. How much of a disadvantage is the subjective nature of drawing to the production of epigraphic illustrations? How do you think subjectivity can be overcome (assuming you think it can)?

The History of Language
Lecture 10

In the last lecture, we considered the second pillar of decipherment: the need for a large, expertly recorded, and readily accessible corpus. In this lecture, we investigate the third pillar: the central importance of language. All languages change; thus, in a sense, ancient writing systems are moving targets. But the very fact of language change makes it possible for linguists to roll back the clock and predict, often in surprising detail, what earlier stages of languages looked like. This ability, too, is a tremendous boon to decipherment.

Ancient Sumerian
- Imagine that archaeologists excavating an ancient city discover tablets at least 5,000 years old. And imagine that on these tablets are inscribed thousands of unfamiliar pictographic characters. Clearly, it's a mixed writing system, but it's so old and so different from any other writing system that decipherment seems hopeless.

- Eventually, after patient work by generations of scholars, it slowly becomes clear that this ancient writing system is ancestral to later ones in the same region. Although these later scripts are less pictorial—because their signs became conventionalized over time—scholars can trace their origins to the signs in these ancient tablets. The comparison allows the meanings of some of these ancient signs to be worked out.

- Later traditions shed some light on the names of the ancient cities and rulers mentioned on the early tablets. One ancient city seems to have been called Warka or Erech. A bilingual inscription is found, and the phonetic values of many signs become apparent, as well as the pronunciations and meanings of a dozen words. The name of the ancient city turns out to be Uruk, with a semi-legendary king named Gilgamesh. Other words, such as *lugal* ("king") and *dingir* ("god"), emerge from the mute past.

- Of course, this situation isn't imaginary at all. It describes the decipherment of Sumerian, a language of ancient Mesopotamia. The Sumerians developed one of the earliest civilizations, but their language passed out of existence as a spoken tongue almost 4,000 years ago. Fortunately, even while Sumerian was dying out, it was being extensively recorded by neighbors of the Sumerians, the Akkadians.

- The early Akkadians had been conquered by Sumer and had adopted its writing system. Eventually, however, they adapted this script to write Akkadian. The Akkadians continued to write prestigious Sumerian alongside their own language for many centuries, even after they had conquered the Sumerians themselves and contributed to the demise of the Sumerian language.

- Akkadian is also a dead language, but because Akkadian was a Semitic language closely related to Arabic and Hebrew, scholars have had a much easier time deciphering the Akkadian script. The decipherment of Sumerian rests largely on the decipherment of Akkadian, and our knowledge of the Sumerian language equally depends on the dictionaries and grammars written by the early Akkadians.
  - To study Sumerian, scholars must first master Semitic and Akkadian. Only then can they turn from the Akkadian dictionaries and grammars to the still more ancient Sumerian texts themselves. When a word or grammatical construction isn't explained in any of the Akkadian descriptions, Sumerian scholars still debate its precise meaning, and the definitions of uncommon words are often not known.

  - This highlights the centrality of language to decipherment. When the underlying language isn't known, decipherment is impossible.

Reconstructing an Ancient Language
- All ancient languages are now dead in one sense or another. Either they have simply vanished, or they have continued to be spoken

over millennia, gradually changing into different languages, as was the case with Classical Latin.

○ Latin attained a remarkable geographic spread during the height of the Roman Empire, and after the fall of Rome in the 5th century A.D., various dialects of vernacular Latin continued to be spoken in many regions, eventually transforming into the modern Romance languages, including Italian, Spanish, Portuguese, and French.

○ No language can survive without change. Even the Ecclesiastical Latin preserved by the Roman Catholic Church has undergone so many changes in words, grammar, and pronunciation since classical times that it would not be instantly recognizable to Caesar or Cicero.

○ Yet Latin is rightly considered one of the best known of all ancient languages. We have thousands of monuments and texts produced by Classical Latin authors. And, as was the case with Sumerian, the Roman alphabet and Latin language were adopted by numerous later groups.

○ If we didn't have any later records, the preservation of Ecclesiastical Latin alone would be more than sufficient to recover most of the nuances of Classical Latin texts. Even without Ecclesiastical Latin, it would still be possible to reconstruct much of Latin on the basis of careful comparison of the Romance family of languages, all descended from a vernacular version of Latin spoken in the streets of Rome and in the Roman provinces.

• Historical linguists long ago worked out the means by which the comparison of related languages could allow the reconstruction of their shared ancestor. This methodology, known as the *comparative method* of linguistic reconstruction, is now a well-developed science.

Case Study in the Comparative Method

- The table below shows the words *goat*, *head*, *meat*, and *dog* in four Romance languages.

English	Italian	Spanish	Portuguese	French	Latin
goat	*capra*	*cabra*	*cabra*	*chèvre*	*capra*
head, top	*capo*	*cabo*	*cabo*	*chef*	*caput*
meat, flesh	*carne*	*carne*	*carne*	*charn*	*carn-*
dog	*cane*	*can*	*cão*	*chien*	*canis*

Assuming that we didn't have the Latin originals, how would a historical linguist go about a reconstruction? First, note that all of these words begin with a /k/ sound in Italian, Spanish, and Portuguese but a /ʃ/ sound in French.

- Actually, the French words used to begin with a /tʃ/ sound, spelled with the letters *ch* (which signal /tʃ/ in most European languages). It seems logical to argue that the original /k/ sound was retained in Italian, Spanish, and Portuguese but changed to /tʃ / and, later, /ʃ/ in French.

- In studying and classifying sound changes over hundreds of years, linguists have established that the change from /k/ to /tʃ/ to /ʃ/ is a common one, known as palatalization, in which a sound moves forward in the mouth. The /k/ sound also shifts from a ***plosive*** to a ***fricative***.

- In fact, we have several good reasons to suggest that the first sound in the Latin word for "goat" would have been /k/. More than that, we can also say that wherever Latin had a /k/ sound, we should expect to see it reflected as Italian /k/ and French /ʃ/. The sounds of a mother tongue are systematically reflected in its descendants.

- We can follow the same reasoning to reconstruct the vowels of the word for "goat" as /a/, similar to the first vowel in our word *father*. French is again the outlier, with /ɛ/ in each of these cases, but we allow the majority to rule once again and reconstruct /a/.

- With the second consonant of the word for "goat," things become a little more complex, because we are comparing /p/, /b/, and /v/.
  - The sound /b/ is what linguists call a voiced **bilabial** plosive; /p/ is a voiceless bilabial plosive. Commonly, voiceless sounds gain **voice** by infection from other voiced sounds nearby.

  - Note that in the Latin word *capra*, there is a preceding /a/ and a following /r/, both of which are voiced. The original /p/ was probably retained in Italian, but it became infected by the surrounding voiced sounds in Spanish and Portuguese to become /b/.

  - French seems to have changed /p/ to /f/ first before voicing /f/ to /v/.

- We can follow a similar approach with the other sounds in these words. It's clear that a fair amount of the Latin original can be reconstructed, although there are also a few gaps in what we can confidently reconstruct in this way.

- If neither Ecclesiastical Latin nor any of the Romance languages existed, at least a partial reconstruction of Classical Latin would still be possible because Latin is a member of the well-known Indo-European language family. Since the early 19th century, historical linguists have been able to compare these related languages using methods similar to those we applied to the Romance languages.

The Evolution of Language
- Until the late 18th century, languages were generally assumed to be fairly static entities, and most scholars, in part because of the influence of the church, tended to trace all languages, even Latin and Greek, back to Hebrew. The scholar Sir William Jones was the

first to make the observation that Latin, Greek, and Sanskrit were so similar that they must "have sprung from some common source, which, perhaps, no longer exists."

○ As it turns out, Proto-Indo-European was the ancestor of Latin, Greek, and Sanskrit in the same way that Latin was the ancestor of Italian, Spanish, Portuguese, and French.

○ Hebrew belongs to a completely different family of languages, Proto-Semitic.

• Such central discoveries of historical linguistics coincided with Charles Darwin's discovery of biological evolution. Darwin's evidence, too, came from the comparison of related organisms and the central insight that related species don't spring directly from one another. Rather, as with sister languages, they must have sprung from some common source that often no longer exists.

• The similarities between the historical development of languages and biological evolution are striking, and they probably apply to all things that reproduce with small, cumulative changes over time. For this reason, there are additional useful parallels. Both historical linguists and evolutionary biologists use comparative

The biblical story of the Tower of Babel explains the diversity of the world's languages by tracing them to a punishment from God to "confound the language of all the earth."

evidence, vestigial features, and fossils to trace developments in their respective fields.

- ○ Consider the English word *knight*. Comparative evidence connects it to German *Knecht* and Dutch *knecht*, both meaning "lad, servant, soldier." Clearly, English lost the original initial /k/and the medial fricative /x/, still present in the continental forms.

- ○ Although **k-n-i-gh-t** is the spelling that survived, texts going back more than 1,000 years offer evidence of several attempts to reflect the earlier sounds, including *c-* before *n* and at least five different ways of indicating the fricative /x/.

- ○ It turns out that all English words spelled with initial *kn-*, such as *knee* and *knot*, were once pronounced with an initial /k/ sound, as revealed by Germanic **cognates**. And it was the loss of the original internal /x/ sound that led to the lengthening of the preceding /i/ to /i:/ and, eventually, its development into the **diphthong** /ai/.

- ○ The vestigial features of the modern English spelling of *knight*, coupled with fossil-like early spellings and comparative evidence from other Germanic languages, help us to trace the development of this word from Old English /knixt/ to Middle English /ni:t/ to Modern English /nait/.

- • Viewing writing systems as fossilized language is a powerful conceptual tool. Written forms give us a material, enduring landmark in a constantly shifting linguistic landscape.

Important Terms

bilabial: Refers to a sound made by pressing both lips together (e.g., *p*, *b*, and *m*).

cognate: The similarity of words in two different languages due to chance, to one language borrowing a word from the other, or to shared descent from a common ancestor, in which case the words are said to be cognate.

comparative method: The method by which historical linguists compare related words in several related languages (i.e., cognates) in order to deduce the form and meaning of a word in their shared common ancestor.

diphthong: Complex vowels made up of two distinct vowels merged into a single syllable (e.g., the medial vowel *ai* in Modern English *knight*).

fricative: A consonant sound made through continuous expulsion of air past the point of articulation (e.g., *f* and *sh* [š]).

plosive (also **stop**): A consonant sound made by briefly building up pressure behind the point of articulation and then releasing it, as in *p*, *b*, and *k*.

voicing: Refers to the vibration of the vocal cords in the production of various sounds, such as vowels and the voiced consonants *b*, *d*, and *g*.

Suggested Reading

Campbell, *Historical Linguistics*.

Darwin, *On the Origin of Species*.

Jones, "Third Anniversary Discourse."

Quilter, Zender, et al., "Traces of a Lost Language and Number System Discovered on the North Coast of Peru."

Questions to Consider

1. The British philologist Ernest Weekley long ago observed that "[s]tability in language is synonymous with *rigor mortis*." In light of what you learned about the history of Latin in this lecture, what do you think Weekley meant?

2. Why do you think words change their pronunciation and meaning over time? Is this a good thing? Why or why not?

3. Given our spellings of such words as *knight* and *knot*, do you think our writing system is in need of reform? Why or why not?

Proper Nouns and Cultural Context
Lecture 11

More than 50 years ago, the distinguished Hittite scholar and grammatologist Johannes Friedrich concluded his book on decipherment with these important words: "[N]othing can be deciphered out of nothing." We have already seen that epigraphers can learn a surprising amount about an ancient script merely by gathering a sufficiently large number of texts and paying close attention to the behavior of signs. But without external evidence of some kind, decipherment can progress no further. Sign frequencies and patterns of an ancient script must be related to something—language, cultural context, or a bilingual—to give us access to their contents. In this lecture, we will continue our thematic exploration of decipherment with a consideration of cultural context.

Proper Nouns and Decipherment

- As mentioned in an earlier lecture, the term *cultural context*, as it relates to decipherment, refers to the idea that traditions and histories giving the names of places, ethnic groups, individuals, and gods should be independently known. These provide an important target for decipherment, which has always exploited the presence of proper names written phonetically.

- Many of our earliest inscriptions tend to record proper names. At the same time, nametags recording the ownership of objects and captions labeling figures in ancient art are among the most common types of ancient inscriptions. This means that names are frequently encountered in ancient writing systems.

- Recall, too, that all writing systems have some phonetic signs, and that proper nouns are usually recorded with those phonetic signs. The main reason for this is that names, whether of people, places, or things, tend to be traditional and archaic. In fact, most names no longer have any clear meaning apart from being names.

○ In ancient times, of course, some names were written logographically. The name of the Aztec emperor Ahuitzotl is a good example. Ahuitzotl means "otter," and his name-glyph is just a pictorially derived logogram for "otter."

○ But most names used phonetic signs, either in whole or in part. In particular, older names whose meanings were lost were often written with phonetic signs.

• When cultures came into contact, foreign names or titles, with their strange sounds and unfamiliar meanings, were also written phonetically.

○ For instance, Champollion's initial decipherments of Egyptian hieroglyphs came mostly from the names and titles of the Ptolemaic Greek rulers of Egypt and the somewhat later names and titles of Roman emperors.

○ Today, scholars are using the names and titles of Spanish conquistadors, missionaries, and colonial governors to decipher Aztec hieroglyphic writing. Clearly, few of these foreign names and titles would have been served by indigenous logograms; thus, phonetic signs were pressed into service to record them.

Herodotus of Halicarnassus

• The ancient Greek historian Herodotus was born in the Greek colony of Halicarnassus, Caria (modern-day Turkey), in about 484 B.C. He was the son of an influential family and seems to have been both well-educated and well-traveled. He also seems to have been caught up in the pronounced political turmoil of his times.

○ Herodotus's hometown of Halicarnassus was a Dorian Greek colony, but it had been conquered and annexed by the Achaemenid Empire of Persia in the mid-6th century B.C., and it was a tribute-paying client of Persia during Herodotus's childhood.

○ Herodotus and his family seem to have been involved in several uprisings against a local Persian quisling and were apparently exiled to Samos before returning to assist in deposing the tyrant. In his late 30s, Herodotus relocated to Athens. There, he wrote his famous *Histories* in about 425 B.C.

The 5th-century-B.C. historian Herodotus is the source of much of our information for the cultural context of Old World writing systems.

- Given Herodotus's background, it seems logical that he would write about the major events of his times. His particular focus in his writing was on the rise of the Persian Empire and the conflict known as the Greco-Persian Wars between the Achaemenid Empire and the Greek city-states during the first half of the 5th century B.C.

- Herodotus not only lived through these wars, but he traveled to many of the key sites mentioned in his books, conducting interviews and collecting stories to amplify his accounts. Herodotus's researches are gathered in his masterful nine-volume account, simply known as *The Histories*.

- *The Histories* are the oldest surviving works of Greek prose, and they report Herodotus's systematic investigation into the origins, development, and conclusion of the wars between Greece and Persia, including numerous details of the people involved; the geography of Greece, Asia Minor, Mesopotamia, and Egypt; and the cultures, customs, and history of the inhabitants of almost the entire known world in Herodotus's day.

- Cicero once called Herodotus the "father of history," but more recent scholars have called him the "father of comparative anthropology" for his discussions of the cultural practices and beliefs of many different foreign peoples. In the study of writing systems, Herodotus contributed much of what we know about the cultural context of the ancient Old World. The decipherers of Egyptian hieroglyphs, cuneiform, and Linear B all leaned heavily on the work of Herodotus in helping them relate the known to the unknown.

  ○ As just one example among many of the incredible utility of Herodotus's *Histories*, consider the famous list of the Seven Wonders of the Ancient World. Herodotus was the first to compile such a list, although the list as we have it today actually comes to us from Antipater of Sidon in about 140 B.C.

  ○ Herodotus's account of the Great Pyramid of Giza tells us that it was constructed as the funeral pyramid of the pharaoh Kheops and goes on to recount the building of the other Giza pyramids by Kheops's son Khephren and Khephren's son Mykerinos. The names of these early pharaohs are precisely the kinds of evidence that Champollion seized on in his decipherment of Egyptian hieroglyphs.

- It's important to note that there are some potential difficulties with this kind of evidence. The names *Kheops*, *Khephren*, and *Mykerinos* are all Hellenized; that is, they are phonetic approximations of early Egyptian names using the Greek alphabet and pronunciation. In popular usage, they've even been Latinized in their spellings and Anglicized in their pronunciations, such that we now write *Cheops* and *Chephren* with an initial *C* and *Mycerinus* with an internal *c* and *u*.

Fourth-Dynasty Pharaohs

- Manethon (or Manetho) was an Egyptian historian and priest from Sebennytos, an ancient city in the Nile delta. He lived in the 3rd century B.C. and wrote a three-volume history of Egypt in the Greek language, known as the *Aegyptiaca*. It provides the basic chronology and division of rulers into dynasties that scholars still follow today.

- Herodotus and Manethon didn't agree on the names of two of the early pharaohs who built the pyramids at Giza. According to Manethon, Suphis was the name of the builder of the Great Pyramid, and Menkheres was the name of his grandson.

- The following table compares the names of three early pharaohs as written in our earliest Greek accounts with the way they're read by Egyptologists today: Khufu, Khafre, and Menkaure.

Latinized	Herodotus	Manethon	Actual Name
Cheops	Khêops	Súphis	Khufu
Chephren	Khêphren	—	Khafre
Mycerinus	Mykerinos	Menkheres	Menkaure

- The differences between the actual Egyptian names and the names in the Greek and Roman sources are precisely why decipherers must be cautious, carefully comparing different accounts and keeping possible complexities constantly in mind.
  - For example, imagine that epigraphers had interpreted the ancient Egyptian sign for **f** in the names Khufu and Khafre as **p** or even aspirated **p^h** on the basis of the Hellenized and Latinized forms. This might be difficult to correct at first, but as more names were deciphered, such as those of Pepi I, Ptolemy, and Cleopatra, it would soon become clear that a mistake had been made.

  - Note that it was precisely the absence of the sound /f/ in Greek that led the Greeks to replace the Egyptian /f/ with either /p/ or aspirated /p^h/. But as luck would have it, Latin had no aspirated /p^h/ sound; thus, the Romans actually turned this sound back into its original /f/!

○ As the ancient Egyptian language became better known to decipherers in the light of Coptic, its descendant, it would eventually be noted that the sign initially and incorrectly identified as **p** or **pʰ** in fact must have been an **f**.

• Decipherers face the constant hazard that the ancient sources they rely on will provide only approximate forms of names. They must, therefore, have at least some basic knowledge of linguistics and phonology to "outguess" their sources as to the proper form of a foreign name.

Decipherment of New World Writing Systems

• Based on current evidence, there was no contact between the Old and New Worlds prior to the Viking settlement of Newfoundland in about A.D. 1000. And knowledge of the literate civilizations of Mexico came only during the explorations and conquests of Hernán Cortés in 1518–1521. This means not only that the writing systems of the New World are independent of those of the Old but also that none of the classical authors provides any useful information about them.

• The cultural context for Aztec and Mayan writing comes to us from the firsthand accounts of Spanish conquistadors, missionaries, and colonial governors. Most important of these are the accounts of the first Franciscan missionaries, who arrived in New Spain in 1524. They quickly learned the local languages, recognizing that they could not proselytize in either Latin or Spanish, and they produced detailed grammars and dictionaries of these languages.

○ Fray Bernardino de Sahagún (1499–1590) was a Franciscan friar and scholar who compiled a 12-volume account of Aztec history, culture, and mythology, known today as the Florentine Codex. His account is written in both *Nahuatl* (the Aztec language) and Spanish.

○ Fray Diego de Landa (1524–1579) was also a Franciscan friar and eventually became the second archbishop of Yucatán. In about 1565, he authored the invaluable *Account of the Things of*

Yucatán, referring to the peninsula on which the northern Maya cities were located. De Landa provided a thorough account of Maya history and mythology, including a detailed discussion of the workings of the Maya calendar, as well as several bilingual keys on the decipherment of Mayan hieroglyphic writing.

○ Between Sahagún and De Landa, epigraphers had ample cultural context to assist in the decipherment of the Aztec and Mayan writing systems.

Important Term

Nahuatl: The language of the Aztecs and many of their neighbors in Central Mexico. A member of the widespread Uto-Aztecan language family and the language recorded in the Aztec script.

Suggested Reading

Friedrich, *Extinct Languages*.

Murray, "Greek Historians."

Strassler, ed., *The Landmark Herodotus*.

Questions to Consider

1. What did Johannes Friedrich mean when he wrote "nothing can be deciphered out of nothing"?

2. Suppose astronauts were to discover an ancient monument on Mars, inscribed with a lengthy and obviously alien inscription. What would Friedrich say about our chances of ever deciphering it? What would have to change to improve those chances?

Bilinguals, Biscripts, and Other Constraints
Lecture 12

In this lecture, we conclude our thematic investigation of decipherment with an exploration of the fifth pillar. In relating known facts to an unknown writing system, few tools are more critical than the presence of a bilingual, biscript, or similar constraint. It's not just a matter of potentiating decipherment, as we'll see, but also of making a decipherment secure and detailed enough to serve as the foundation for future work. We'll first look at the most famous example of a bilingual, the Rosetta Stone; then, we'll turn to a more general examination of bilinguals, biscripts, and constraints to see how epigraphers use these tools to decipher ancient scripts.

Napoleon's Egyptian Campaign and the Rosetta Stone
- Napoleon Bonaparte's Mediterranean and Egyptian campaign was a phenomenal occurrence in the late 18th century.
    - Capturing Malta on his way to Egypt, Napoleon made landfall in Egypt on July 1, 1798. He immediately pressed his assault against the Mameluke regime of the Ottoman Empire, scoring a signal victory in the Battle of the Pyramids just three weeks later, on July 21. But the French fleet lost the Battle of the Nile against Rear Admiral Sir Horatio Nelson on August 1–3, 1798.

    - Word of the British victories seemed to undermine Napoleon's popular support in France, and he left Egypt in August 1799. Within two years, Malta had been retaken by the British, and the Napoleonic Fort St. Julien at al-Rashid was besieged and subjected to a four-day bombardment.

    - The French capitulated on August 31, 1801. The British controlled Egypt, and many of the antiquities collected by the French were seized by the British navy, eventually ending up in the British Museum.

- Napoleon's campaign was primarily a military venture, designed to protect French trade interests against the Ottomans and to secure a strategic base from which to undermine British access to India. On both of those fronts, it failed miserably. But on the cultural and historical front, Napoleon's expedition remains an unqualified success, still heralded in the annals of discovery.

- A brilliant propagandist and true student of the Enlightenment, Napoleon had hidden some of his imperial ambitions by taking along a veritable army of scholars to study Egyptian geology, flora and fauna, languages, architecture, and archaeology. The expedition's discoveries were published in the 19-volume *Description de l'Egypte*. Its most celebrated discovery was the Rosetta Stone.

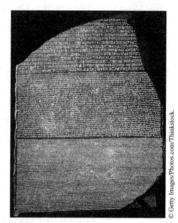

Captured after the naval bombardment of al-Rashid, the Rosetta Stone was hauled off to Britain as a spoil of conquest; it can be seen in the British Museum today.

  o The Rosetta Stone was discovered in mid-July 1799, embedded in the support wall of a Mameluke fortress at al-Rashid. It contains three different writing systems. The bottom section is in the well-known Greek alphabet. The damaged upper section is written in Egyptian hieroglyphs, and the central section is written in what was, at the time, the practically unknown *demotic* script.

  o The only part of the written message that could be made out at first was the well-preserved Greek text, but its inscription implied that the hieroglyphic and demotic texts conveyed the same message as the Greek. The bilingual key provided by the Rosetta Stone enabled numerous early scholars to make progress in deciphering hieroglyphs, culminating in the work of Jean-François Champollion.

Bilingual Decrees in the Ancient World

- Despite the stories that would like to give credit for the Rosetta Stone to aliens, time travelers, or even Napoleon himself, it isn't an unlikely artifact at all. And although it's undoubtedly iconic and important, the Rosetta Stone isn't the only Egyptian bilingual.

  o The text on the Rosetta Stone itself indicates that it was but one of a large number of copies intended to be set up in temples throughout the cities of the Nile delta, though thus far, only parts of two others have been discovered.

  o Further, at least two earlier bilingual decrees are known: the Canopus decree of Ptolemy III (238 B.C.) and the Memphis decree of Ptolemy IV (c. 218 B.C.). Another famous Egyptian bilingual is the Bankes obelisk, which contains the names of Cleopatra III in Greek and Egyptian. In all, there are more than a dozen bilinguals and biscripts relating Egyptian to other languages and writing systems.

  o Nor are bilinguals and biscripts a uniquely Egyptian phenomenon. They are actually fairly common wherever two or more literate traditions overlap in time and space. Thus, the famous Behistun inscription of Darius the Great records the great emperor's conquests in his own tongue, Achaemenid Persian, as well as Babylonian and Elamite. In the Mediterranean, the golden Pyrgi tablets record a temple dedication in both Etruscan and Phoenician.

- There seem to be several reasons for the proliferation of bilinguals. The Rosetta Stone was a royal decree, intended to be published throughout Egypt in all of the most important temples. It established the divine cult of the new ruler, Ptolemy V; granted a tax exemption to the resident priesthood; and indicated gifts that were to be made to the temples. In this context, the use of three distinct writing systems had both traditional and practical motivations.

o   The hieroglyphs were explicitly the "language of the gods"; their use reflected the temple setting of the decrees. Demotic was the language of documents, and its use helped to establish the official status of the Rosetta Stone's proclamations. Finally, the Greek language was used by the Ptolemies themselves and was the international language of the 2nd century B.C.

o   The need or desire to communicate information across complex, multilingual environments also explains many of the bilinguals that have come down to us today. The great trilingual inscriptions of the Achaemenid Empire served the practical purpose of communicating the needs and wants of the Achaemenids to a widespread populace, but they also sent a parallel message about the extent of the empire.

o   Asymmetrical cultural contact provides an unmistakable context for the production of other bilinguals, as well. In the New World, there's no doubt that 16th-century bilinguals of Aztec and Mayan writing served colonialist ambitions to describe and circumscribe the indigenous population. Without them, we would perhaps never have deciphered these writing systems, yet we nonetheless recognize that these precious documents served as conquerors' tools.

Multilinguals and Multiscripts

- The term *bilingual* refers to an object that bears two different languages, regardless of whether or not they are recorded in one or two writing systems. The term *biscript*, in contrast, refers to an object with two different writing systems, regardless of whether or not they record one or two languages.

- Thus, a single object with two parallel texts can be both a bilingual and a biscript. An object with parallel texts in two different languages but using the same writing system is a bilingual, but it's a uniscript, not a biscript. An object with two parallel texts written in the same language but using two different scripts is a biscript, but it's a unilingual, not a bilingual.

- This terminology can also be extended to contexts where more than two parallel texts are involved, giving us such terms as trilingual and triscript, quadrilingual and quadriscript, and so forth.

- Examples of bilingual uniscripts include street signs in both French and English in Canada and in Dutch and French in Brussels. In Hong Kong, the street signs are bilingual biscripts; they show the Cantonese language in Chinese characters alongside the English language in the Roman alphabet. The Rosetta Stone is a bilingual triscript, because the hieroglyphs and the demotic effectively record the same Egyptian language.

- The concept of bilinguals and biscripts is a common one in the modern world and is found in ancient civilizations, as well. This is good news for epigraphers because bilinguals remain the keystones of all successful decipherment. Not only do they make decipherment possible in the first place, but they also provide one of the few sure ways for epigraphers to both derive and test their posited sign values, increasing the certainty of their decipherments.

The Value of Bilinguals and Constraints
- In the last lecture, we saw that names are a critical component of many decipherments, and they loom large in the context of bilinguals, as well, because they provide a ready control for the sound values of signs. In decipherment, we aim first and foremost to account for the functions of signs, and names within a bilingual context provide the most economical way of getting at this information.

- It isn't strictly the case that a script cannot be deciphered without a bilingual. The first steps toward the decipherment of Old Persian, Hittite hieroglyphics, and the Ugaritic alphabet were all taken without a bilingual. That said, bilinguals have since been found for all of these scripts, and in each case, the initially posited values for signs were significantly revised, placing the decipherments of these systems on a much firmer footing.

- Of all the better-known decipherments, only Michael Ventris's decipherment of Myecenaean Linear B, the ancient writing system of Crete, was truly pursued without a bilingual inscription.
  - Archaeologists still haven't found either a bilingual or a biscript for Linear B, but this script has a historical relationship with the *Cypriotic syllabary* from the nearby island of Cyprus. Ventris (1922–1956) was able to exploit this relationship to confirm certain sign values. We call these relationships *constraints*, because they set helpful limitations on the decipherment of related scripts.

  - Similarly, Linear B contains a kind of "internal biscript" that provided a second constraint for Ventris's decipherment. That is, the script has a large number of semantic signs that serve to define the basic meanings of associated words spelled with syllabic signs.

  - Linear B still remains poorly known, with several signs of unknown value and more with uncertain or speculative values. Should a bilingual or biscript ever be discovered, it's inevitable that it would force some refinements on the current state of the decipherment.

- Historical relationships between scripts are important constraints for epigraphers. As mentioned, Linear B and Cypriotic have some relationship, although it's not known whether Cypriotic was borrowed from Linear B or whether both descended from a predecessor script. In any case, the potential to decipher an unknown writing system on the basis of related writing systems not only exists but has been used to good effect in the decipherment of various related cuneiform scripts, such as Sumerian and Hittite, both deciphered largely on the basis of Babylonian.

- Picture biscripts represent another important kind of constraint. These are texts that appear in close association with an image, as a kind of caption, title, or gloss. Etruscan mirror backs are an excellent context for this kind of constraint, where recognizable images of Greek gods, goddesses, and heroes are associated with short captions providing their names. Picture biscripts have also proven themselves to be critical constraints in the decipherments of both Mayan and Aztec hieroglyphic writing.

Important Terms

Cypriotic script (or **Cypriotic syllabary**): A syllabary from Cyprus, recording a dialect of ancient Greek and dating to c. 800–250 B.C. This script is related to both Linear A and Linear B.

demotic: A visually simplified Egyptian logophonetic script developed in the 7th century B.C. One of the three scripts on the Rosetta Stone.

Suggested Reading

Adkins and Adkins, *The Keys of Egypt*.

Friedrich, *Extinct Languages*.

McLuhan, *Understanding Media*.

Parkinson, *The Rosetta Stone*.

Piper, "Omnilingual."

Robinson, *Cracking the Egyptian Code*.

Tierney, "Who Should Own the Rosetta Stone?"

1. Is the Rosetta Stone "too good to be true"? Why or why not?

2. Who should own the Rosetta Stone? Consider the arguments in favor of ownership by Britain and France, as well as those for repatriation to Egypt.

Egyptian—The First Great Decipherment
Lecture 13

Almost two centuries ago, Jean-François Champollion played a major role in the decipherment of Egyptian hieroglyphs, a writing system that had been lost for 1,300 years. Why were Egyptian history, the Egyptian language, and even the workings of this remarkable hieroglyphic writing system so completely forgotten by the West? Why, following the rediscovery of Egyptian civilization during the Renaissance, did it take so long until these things were recovered? What guesses and evidence led Champollion—alone among all his contemporaries and predecessors—down the correct path to decipherment? And what was learned from the decipherment of Egyptian hieroglyphs that could not have been figured out in any other way? We'll explore these questions in this lecture.

Lost Knowledge

- For more than three millennia, Egypt was an imperial civilization of millions of people, its writings filling millions of papyrus scrolls and carved on thousands of monuments. It fought wars with other nations, forged alliances, and engaged in widespread trade and diplomatic communication. Yet much of our knowledge of it vanished for some 1,300 years.

- One reason the loss of our knowledge of Egypt is counterintuitive is that Egypt was well known in antiquity. The great historian Herodotus wrote about Egypt in the middle of the 5th century B.C., as did Manethon of Sebennytos and Pliny the Elder in later times. Julius Caesar and Mark Antony both sojourned in Egypt in the mid-1st century B.C. The lesson here is that fame is not the same thing as immortality.

- What happened to Egypt? The simple answer is that it was conquered—many times, in wave after wave of invasion and occupation, until it simply succumbed, adopting the language, writing, and culture of its conquerors. Egypt's long era of sovereignty ended in 525 B.C., when it was conquered by the Achaemenid Persians under Cambyses.

- Egypt remained part of the Persian Empire for the next two centuries, and Herodotus tells us that Egyptian archers fought with the Persian army against Athenians and Spartans at the battles of Marathon, Thermopylae, and Plataea.

- Alexander the Great wrested Egypt from Persian control in 332 B.C. After Alexander's death, his best friend and general, Ptolemy, took control of Egypt. He eventually crowned himself king and inaugurated the Macedonian Greek Ptolemaic dynasty, which ruled until the death of Cleopatra VII in 30 B.C. The Romans then occupied Egypt for more than 400 years, until the rise of Christianity and Coptic Christian rule in the late 4th century A.D.

- The great library of Alexandria, storehouse of so much Egyptian history, was burned to the ground at this time under Christian edict. In the pogrom against paganism that followed, many Egyptian temples were converted to Coptic Christian temples, and the hieroglyphic characters, so closely associated with pagan religion, were abandoned. Replacing the hieroglyphs was the Coptic alphabet, a script derived from the Greek alphabet, with 30 characters for consonants and vowels.

- Arab invaders occupied Christian Egypt in A.D. 642, introducing the Arabic language and the religion of Islam. This led to still more pogroms and, in short order, to the adoption of Arabic and the demise of Coptic as an everyday spoken language. Coptic continued to exist only in the liturgical tradition of the Coptic Christian Church.

Erroneous Conclusions about Egyptian
- Neither Greek nor Roman scholars bothered to learn either the Egyptian language or any of its indigenous writing systems. What's more, in the absence of authentic ancient knowledge of hieroglyphs, early writers tended to concoct their own "facts." The early Greek

historian Diodorus Siculus, for example, wrote, "Egyptian writing was not built up from syllables to express the underlying meaning, but from the appearance of things drawn and by their metaphorical meaning learned by heart."

- The 4th-century-A.D. Egyptian writer Horapollo forced the few fragmentary bits of genuine lore that came down to him to fit Siculus's notions about hieroglyphs as metaphorical picture writing rather than actual writing. Unfortunately, Horapollo's writings were rediscovered and republished in 1505 and became wildly popular. Horapollo's central idea, that Egyptian hieroglyphs spoke directly to the mind without taking a detour through the Egyptian language, became the unshakable belief of many for the next 300 years.

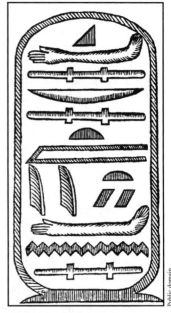

Public domain

Kircher had privileged access to Egyptian inscriptions in Rome, including an obelisk commissioned by the emperor Domitian in the 1st century A.D., but he still managed to bungle his decipherment badly.

- In the 17th century, the Jesuit priest Athanasius Kircher published the first European grammar and vocabulary of the endangered Coptic language, but strangely, he never noticed that Coptic was itself the descendant of the ancient Egyptian language. Champollion would later use Kircher's Coptic grammar to make precisely this discovery, demonstrating that Coptic *etymology* could explain the few scraps of Egyptian vocabulary that had survived in the works of such classical authors as Herodotus, Manethon, and Pliny.

Breakthrough of the Egyptian Expedition

- The turning point for Egyptian came with Napoleon Bonaparte's invasion of Egypt in 1798–1801. As we saw in the previous lecture, Napoleon's expedition not only uncovered the Rosetta Stone, but it also led to the publication of the multivolume work titled the *Description de l'Egypte*, which appeared in print between 1809 and 1828.

- With the publication of the final volume, scholars immediately set to work to decipher the hieroglyphs.
  - Noting that the names Alexander, Alexandria, and Ptolemy all appear in the Greek text on the Rosetta Stone, scholars reasoned that they should expect these names to appear in the demotic text, as well.

  - Egyptian writing was thought to record ideas rather than sounds, but many scholars assumed that the Egyptians would have had no choice but to use some of the signs in their popular demotic script in a phonetic way when confronted with foreign sounds, such as those in Macedonian Greek names.

  - This assumption was true enough, but as we'll see, the implication of this reasoning—that the Egyptians wouldn't write their own names phonetically—was both unjustified and incorrect.

- By comparing the better-preserved demotic text to the Greek and by following the assumption that the most frequently repeating element in the former would be Ptolemy's name, early scholars were able to isolate the Ptolemy sequence in the text. Then, on the assumption of general equivalency to Greek alphabetic values, they drew up tentative alphabets for demotic.
  - The problem, of course, is that demotic is not an alphabet. Like the hieroglyphs, it's a mixed logophonetic script.

- o   As a result, early scholars stumbled whenever the signs they were examining represented words rather than just sounds, or when they identified signs for vowels (which don't exist).

- o   Unfortunately, these early scholars took their difficulties as confirming rather than challenging what they had imbibed from their classical training. They could not bring themselves to believe that all those pictures of hawks, crocodiles, and geese conveyed sounds rather than ideas.

The Work of Champollion

- •   It was into this heady period that Jean-François Champollion (1790–1832) was born in a small town in southwestern France. As a youth, Champollion was captivated by Napoleon's discoveries in Egypt. In 1808, he received a high-quality copy of the Rosetta Stone inscription and began to work on deciphering the hieroglyphs, an effort that would take him more than 14 years.

- •   In the beginning, Champollion made the same comparisons that earlier scholars had made between the Greek and the better-preserved demotic texts. Eventually, it occurred to him to simply count the signs of the Egyptian and demotic texts, though here, he ran into the same difficulty that had hampered earlier researchers: The hieroglyphs of the Rosetta Stone were incomplete. What he needed was a part of the hieroglyphic text that he could directly compare to the demotic and Greek to ensure that his comparison started in the same place.

- •   Champollion identified a repeating element in the hieroglyphic text: an oval encircling several hieroglyphs. The earlier scholar Thomas Young had suggested that these *cartouches* contained the name of Ptolemy.
  - o   Champollion used this as his benchmark, counting the hieroglyphs from the last cartouche to the end of the text and comparing them with the number of signs from the last occurrence of the name Ptolemy in the demotic text.

- He found that they were more or less the same and came to realize that the scripts were really variants of each other: the hieroglyphs, a formal script reserved for monuments; the demotic, a cursive script for correspondence.

- This led to a further insight. Given that many authorities accepted that the demotic script recorded foreign names phonetically because of their strange sounds, the hieroglyphics must have had recourse to the same principle. Counting the number of signs in the hieroglyphic cartouches and relating them to the demotic signs spelling the name Ptolemy, Champollion was convinced that the name Ptolemy, at least, was being rendered by sound signs. He tested this idea by examining numerous other cartouches from Egyptian monuments dating to the Ptolemaic and Roman periods.

- Champollion was able to read the Greek title *autocrator* ("ruler") and some Greek and Roman names, but he still labored under the assumption that only the names and titles of foreigners, enclosed in cartouches, involved hieroglyphs operating phonetically. He believed that the hundreds of other *glyphs* stood for ideas.

- The next breakthrough came when Champollion received the final volume of the *Description de l'Egypte*, with its detailed plates of the inscriptions of Ramses II, Tuthmosis III, and other pharaohs of the 18th and 19th dynasties. The names of these pharaohs had been recorded by Manethon and Herodotus, and Champollion quickly recognized that the same phonetic signs he had discovered in Greek- and Roman-era inscriptions provided their names in cartouches.
  - Based on his knowledge of Coptic, Champollion knew that the name of Ramses was thoroughly Egyptian, meaning "the sun god is born." It could no longer be argued that Egyptian hieroglyphs transcribed only foreign names phonetically. The principle was, in fact, an ancient one and had merely been put to new use to record the names of foreigners.

  - Nevertheless, Champollion attempted to explain away his own discovery, arguing that perhaps it was the category of names that explained this usage. The inscriptions outside the cartouches, he believed, still communicated ideas rather than sounds.

- The early 1820s found Champollion working around the clock to solve the problem of the Egyptian hieroglyphs. Then, one night, he had a eureka moment. In the text outside the cartouches, he finally recognized an early form of Coptic. Champollion now knew exactly how the signs outside the cartouches functioned to provide the same message written in the long-understood Greek text.

- With his brother's help, Champollion quickly prepared his insights for publication. In his *Lettre à M. Dacier*, he published his famous alphabetic table of hieroglyphs. He would eventually write grammars and dictionaries of Egyptian, although he died only 10 years after his epochal decipherment, at 41 years of age.

Important Terms

cartouche: An oval encircling a group of Egyptian hieroglyphs and providing one of the names of the pharaoh.

etymology: The origin of a word and the historical development of its meaning.

glyph: A convenient term for signs in any hieroglyphic script, abbreviated from hieroglyph.

Suggested Reading

Adkins and Adkins, *The Keys of Egypt*.

Meyerson, *The Linguist and the Emperor*.

Robinson, *Cracking the Egyptian Code*.

1. Given that all of the pillars of decipherment were in place before Champollion and that Silvestre de Sacy, Johan Åkerblad, and Thomas Young had all preceded him in identifying the crucial Ptolemy cartouche on the Rosetta Stone, what was Champollion's signal contribution to the decipherment of Egyptian? What qualities do you suppose made it possible for him to make this breakthrough?

2. Do you think Western civilization could ever become as completely forgotten as Egypt was? Why or why not?

What Do Egyptian Hieroglyphs Say?
Lecture 14

In the Brooklyn Museum of Art, there is a small, fragmentary wall panel from the mortuary temple of Hatshepsut in Deir el Bahari, Thebes. The panel is only about six inches high, but like much of Egyptian art, it represents a world in a grain of sand. Eight glyphs and two fragmentary images tell a compelling story about a lost world. How was this lost world of meaning recovered? In the last lecture, we saw how difficult it was for Champollion to overcome the entrenched dogma that ancient Egyptian was an ideographic script, even in the presence of all five pillars of decipherment. In this lecture, we'll look at the contexts that first suggested values for individual Egyptian signs.

A Fragment from Deir el Bahari

- A 3,500-year-old fragment from the mortuary temple of Hatshepsut depicts a king wearing the so-called blue crown (or *khepresh*). A large cartouche to the right of this figure encircles three hieroglyphs giving the royal name Tuthmosis III.

- From top to bottom, the signs represent a solar disk (**rʿ**), a chess-like game shown in profile (**mn**), and a scarab beetle (**ḫpr**). All three of these signs are logograms, and they can be read as Menkheperre, the royal name taken by Tuthmosis III when he came to the throne.

- Notice that the solar disk sign, **rʿ**, is read last, even though it appears at the top of the column of signs. This is a tricky feature of Egyptian writing called *honorific transposition*. The solar sign is moved up in the text to honor it, but it's still read last.

- Remember that Egyptian writing does not record vowels. Thus, the solar disk conveys only /r/ and a voiced ***pharyngeal*** fricative /ʿ/ (similar to Hebrew *'ayin*). Scholars add the *e* of the popular vocalization *re* only to make it easier to discuss these ancient words. In fact, it now seems likely that the ancient Egyptians pronounced this word something like /riʻu:w/. The vowels in *men* and *kheper* are also a convenience, not written by the ancient Egyptians.

- The signs to the right of the cartouche are read from right to left, working toward the profile of the king, and then top to bottom. In fact, they would have immediately preceded the cartouche in a reading of the whole text. Taken together, these signs can be read as meaning "the perfect god, lord of the two lands." This latter title is a traditional one for Egyptian kings, referring to the two lands of Upper and Lower Egypt.

- Although the relief is fragmentary, the figure of the king appears to represent a royal statue, not a portrait, and just enough survives to the right to indicate another royal statue. The image probably depicted a procession of royal statues commemorating an annual festival in Thebes.

A Return to the Rosetta Stone

- Thomas Young was the first to prove that the Rosetta Stone cartouches provided the name of Ptolemy (Greek: Ptolemaios), though his proposal was weakened by the idea that both consonants and vowels would be provided (as in a full alphabet), by several erroneous values even for the consonants, and by his inability to explain why some cartouches contained more signs that others.

- In one of the longer cartouches, simply counting the signs yields 18 separate elements. The shorter cartouches omit the last 11 elements; this suggested to Champollion that some kind of title probably followed the name in the case of the longer cartouches.

- What followed for Champollion was basically a process of trial and error. By proposing certain sound values for these signs (based on the idea that they spelled the name Ptolemaios), the signs could be tested in other contexts, such as the Bankes obelisk, and in other cartouches to see if they continued to yield reasonable results. Through this mechanism, Champollion eventually disproved the idea that any of these signs provided vowels, because they simply could not be sustained with such values in other contexts.

- The values that ultimately proved correct are **p-t-w-l-m-y-s**. Note that consonants alone are written, as is the case throughout the Egyptian writing system. Note also that all of the signs are phonetic, conveying single consonants only. There probably weren't any logograms that would readily capture the barbaric sounds heard by the Egyptians in the Macedonian Greek name Ptolemaios.

- These sign values were greatly strengthened by being substantially the same ones present on the Bankes obelisk, where the hieroglyphic name of Cleopatra overlaps with respect to the signs for **p**, **t**, **l**, and **w**. Using these signs, Champollion went on to read the hieroglyphic names of Alexander the Great and Augustus Caesar, as well as numerous Greek and Latin titles.

- The signs following the name of Ptolemaios mean "immortal" and "beloved of Ptah," an important patron god of Memphis. The whole cartouche thus reads, "Ptolemaios the immortal, beloved of Ptah." The foreign name of this king was written with phonetic signs providing single consonants only, and the more traditional titles of the Egyptian rulers were written in a mixture of logograms, phonetic signs, and semantic signs. It is this mixture that is most representative of Egyptian writing in all periods and is also present in both *hieratic* and demotic.

- Given all the phonetic signs recording single consonants in the names of Ptolemy, Cleopatra, Augustus Caesar, Alexander, and others, it's easy to sympathize with Champollion's presentation of these words as the main "key" to Egyptian writing. However, we now know that there are several errors in Champollion's table of phonetic signs, published in his famous *Lettre à M. Dacier* in 1822.
  ○ These errors shouldn't detract from Champollion's achievement. It bears repeating that decipherment is a process, not a solitary event.

- If later work has been able to show where Champollion was led astray by the late spellings of foreigners' names, then this was only made possible because of the firm foundation on which he placed this field.

Damnatio Memoriae

- Egyptian hieroglyphs were often recarved in a practice scholars call *damnatio memoriae*, Latin for "condemnation of memory." It refers to a well-known punishment of the Roman Senate, usually pronounced against traitors, who were literally erased from historical records. This was much easier to accomplish in the ancient world, when writing was both less common and often under the control of the state.

- *Damnatio memoriae* takes several forms in Egyptian records. The first and most common is the literal recarving of inscriptions. A fragmentary carving from Bubastis, now in the British Museum, shows a partially erased earlier cartouche, of which the elements **ka** and **r'** are all that survive.
  - If the original cartouche was that of Maatkare, then this would have been the throne name of the problematic 18th-dynasty Queen Hatshepsut (r. 1498–1483 B.C.). She was the coregent for her young stepson Tuthmosis III before seizing the throne in her own right.

  - When Tuthmosis III came of age, he toppled many of her statues at Deir el Bahari and erased her name from many monuments. This one escaped him but was partially recarved more than 200 years later with one of the cartouches of the 19th-dynasty pharaoh Ramesses the Great (1279–1212).

- Another kind of *damnatio memoriae* can be seen on the walls of Ramesses II's memorial temple at Abydos, the cult center of Osiris. The middle row of cartouches on an inscription in the memorial provides the names of all the 18th- and 19th-dynasty pharaohs who preceded Ramesses the Great, with the exceptions of Queen Hatshepsut, Akhenaten, and Tutankhamun. The latter two are the pharaohs of the Amarna heresy, who moved the capital from Thebes to Amarna and elevated the cult of the Aten to a monotheistic state religion.

- *Damnatio memoriae* teaches us that Egyptian writing was both a tool and a weapon of the state. Thus, scholars must be cautious in their interpretations of single monuments, drawing their conclusions instead from the careful comparison of many texts from different time periods and a broad region and from archaeological evidence.

The Tomb of Senbi

- In the early 20th century, the Egyptologist Aylward Blackman (1883–1956) investigated a series of rock-cut tombs at Meir in Upper Egypt. One of these tombs was designed for Senbi, a "governor" and "overseer of priests" during the reign of the 12th-dynasty pharaoh Amenemhet I. The tomb was lavishly decorated with carved and painted scenes whose contents bear directly on the Egyptian view of the afterlife.

© iStockphoto/Thinkstock.

Ramesses II's memorial temple at Abydos was excavated in the early 19th century; its impressive list of the kings of Egypt can be seen in the British Museum today.

- One of the main scenes depicts two tall figures, facing each other. Both stand on a small reed boat accompanied by smaller female figures. They float on a stylized River Nile, complete with water plants, reeds, and rushes. The leftmost figure holds out a long spear, on which the bodies of two fish are impaled. The rightmost figure prepares to toss a curved throwing stick at a group of birds in the rushes before him. In his right hand, he holds some captured birds, while the woman below him holds other captured birds.

- The hieroglyphs associated with this scene read as follows: "It is the spearing of fish by the revered one of Osiris, the governor and overseer of priests, Senbi, the justified," and "It is a throwing at birds by the governor, seal-bearer and sole companion of the king, Senbi, the justified." The justification title is important because it predicts that Senbi's soul would manage to avoid the perils of the Egyptian underworld and pass the final judgment of Anubis, where his conscience would be weighed against a feather.

- As we've seen, hieroglyphs provide a rich window into the political organization and religious beliefs of one of the oldest civilizations. Like many writing systems, the Egyptian one is a blend of phonetic signs, logograms, and semantic signs. Most people can easily memorize all the phonetic signs and many of the common semantic signs, enabling them to experience the satisfaction of being able to read words and phrases on an ancient monument.

Important Terms

damnatio memoriae: Latin for "condemnation of memory," referring to a punishment of traitors by the Roman Senate, whose names were stricken from historical records.

hieratic: An early Egyptian logophonetic script designed for painting on papyrus. Replaced in most secular contexts by the demotic script in the 7th century B.C.

pharyngeal: A sound produced by articulating the root of the tongue with the pharynx, as in the Semitic consonant *'ayin*.

Suggested Reading

Blackman, *The Rock Tombs of Meir.*

Bond, "Erasing the Face of History."

Champollion, *Lettre à M. Dacier.*

———, *Précis du système hiéroglyphique des anciens Égyptiens.*

———, *Grammaire Égyptienne, ou principes généraux de l'écriture sacrée Égyptienne.*

Collier and Manley, *How to Read Egyptian Hieroglyphs.*

Fazzini, Romano, and Cody, *Art for Eternity.*

Gardiner, *Egyptian Grammar.*

Kamrin, *Ancient Egyptian Hieroglyphs.*

Lepsius, "*Lettre à M. le Professeur H. Rosellini.*"

Loprieno, *Ancient Egyptian.*

Zauzich, "Hieroglyphs without Mystery."

Questions to Consider

1. What do you think about the preoccupation of the ancient Egyptians with themes of immortality, eternity, and the afterlife? Are these radically different from our own concerns, 3,500 years later? Why or why not?

2. In light of what we've discussed about the inertia of writing systems in earlier lectures, why do you think the ancient Egyptians never abandoned their complex logophonetic writing in favor of an abjad or alphabet?

Old Persian—Cuneiform Deciphered
Lecture 15

In this lecture, we'll meet a high school teacher who made an incomparable contribution to the study of ancient writing and civilization. Georg Grotefend (1775–1853) was a German contemporary of Champollion, a math teacher, and a lover of puzzles. When the cuneiform writing of Mesopotamia began to come to the attention of the European intelligentsia in the late 18th and early 19th centuries, Grotefend recognized a great puzzle worthy of his attention. As we'll see, he came on the scene at exactly the right time, when good drawings of cuneiform inscriptions were just becoming available, along with scholarly analyses of Avestan and Farsi, critical languages for the decipherment of Old Persian.

Cuneiform Scripts

- The term *cuneiform* is Latin and means "wedge shaped." It is used to describe all the writing systems of ancient Mesopotamia, Anatolia, and Persia, because they were formed by pressing the cut end of a reed stylus into wet clay, creating a wedge-shaped impression.

- Some cuneiform scripts are related, while others are not. Old Akkadian, for instance, was derived from Sumerian cuneiform in much the same way that the Japanese *kanji* were derived from Chinese characters. Different groups, such as the Elamites, Babylonians, and others, later borrowed this Akkadian adaptation of Sumerian cuneiform.

- However, not all wedge-shaped scripts have this ancestry. Some, such as the Ugaritic alphabet and the Achaemenid Persian syllabary, were merely inspired by these earlier and contemporary scripts. They had an outward cuneiform appearance but were quite distinct in terms of organization and number of signs.

- As with Chinese and Japanese writing, cuneiform represents a situation in which several writing systems are related, but the languages aren't!

  ○ The Sumerians, who were the inventors of cuneiform, spoke a language that is now extinct, without any surviving relatives. The same is true of the Elamites and Hurrians. The Akkadians, Babylonians, and Assyrians all spoke different but related Semitic languages. Those languages have living relatives, including Modern Hebrew and Arabic.

  ○ The Hittites and the Achaemenid Persians spoke Indo-European languages that were related to each other, albeit distantly, as well as to English, Latin, Greek, and Sanskrit. The Hittite language has no direct descendant, whereas Achaemenid Persian developed into Modern Persian (also known as Farsi).

The ruins of Darius's palace at Persepolis leave no doubt that this colossal structure was once the seat of a mighty empire.

- The three contemporary scripts Achaemenid Elamite, Late Babylonian, and Achaemenid Persian (also known as Old Persian) were all used by the Achaemenid dynasty of Persia during the late 6th century B.C. All three scripts have different origins and represent unrelated languages. The contemporary use of these three scripts made possible the decipherment of Old Persian, as well as Elamite and Babylonian.

The Achaemenid Empire
- The imperial Achaemenid dynasty ruled a great swath of Asia Minor roughly from the mid-6th century B.C., under Cyrus the Great, to the late 4th century B.C., under Darius III.
  - Although the capital of the Achaemenids was at Persepolis, they had conquered Egypt under Cambyses in 525 B.C. and then came into conflict with the Greek colonies of Sardes and Ionia in Asia Minor. These were quickly subjugated, but the Ionian cities revolted with the assistance of Athens, leading Darius I to invade Greece itself, though he was turned back at the Battle of Marathon in 490 B.C.

  - The son of Darius, Xerxes I, attacked Greece some 10 years later, leading to the brave stand of the 300 Spartans at Thermopylae, the sacking of Athens, and the eventual defeat of the Persians at Plataea in 479.

  - The Persians became a traditional enemy of the Greeks until Alexander the Great's short-lived Macedonian Empire at last conquered Persepolis in 330 B.C. Alexander burned the imperial capital to the ground in long-delayed vengeance for Xerxes's sack of Athens.

- Much of what we know about the Achaemenids comes from the writings of Herodotus. Yet despite Alexander's conquest and Herodotus's writings, Western knowledge of Persia effectively disappeared with the Muslim occupation of this region during the 7th century A.D. The rediscovery of Persia began in the early 17th century, when European explorers braved the Ottoman and Persian empires to bring back accounts of great ruins and examples of clay bricks with strange writings.

Establishing the Five Pillars

- Around 1770, the Danish explorer Carsten Niebuhr (1733–1815) made a stop in his travels at Persepolis to copy its inscriptions. Although all of them were cuneiform in outward shape, he nonetheless recognized three different scripts with different numbers and types of signs; he published his drawings in 1772.

- Niebuhr made a number of insightful observations on the script we now call Old Persian. First, given that the script used only about 40 distinct signs, Niebuhr proposed that it was an alphabet. This idea influenced many scholars, including Grotefend, but it was incorrect. Second, Niebuhr was also able to demonstrate that the script read from left to right, and he identified a sign that seemed to operate almost like punctuation between words.

- Several of the pillars of decipherment were already in place by the time Grotefend began working. Accurate copies of the inscriptions of Persepolis were available; the type of script was assumed to be an alphabet; and thanks to Herodotus, the cultural context of the Achaemenids was known. The Persian language was known, and biscripts were available.

The Persian Language

- Modern Persian (or Farsi) is the official language of Iran, where it's spoken by more than 30 million people. An additional 7 million people speak the closely related dialects of Dari and Tajik in Afghanistan and Tajikistan, respectively. These dialects all descend from the Persian spoken by Darius and Xerxes 2,500 years ago.

- Modern Persian is, of course, very different from the language that was carved on the walls at Persepolis, but two factors combined to make Old Persian almost entirely recoverable.
  - First, a group of Persian speakers known as Parsees, practitioners of the religion Zoroastrianism, had preserved

several sacred texts, collectively referred to as the Avesta and dating back to about the 4th century A.D. These texts were translated by the French orientalist A.-H. Anquetil-Duperron in 1771, and the language turned out to be an early form of Persian, effectively bridging the Old Persian writings of the Achaemenids and its modern descendants.

- ○ Second, Persian is an Indo-European language. Specifically, it's in the Indo-Iranian branch of that family, closely grouped with Sanskrit and Hindi, but it's also related to many other well-known ancient and modern languages. For this reason, words in Old Persian can often be reconstructed on the basis of patterned relationships among Avestan, Persian, and other Indo-Iranian languages.

- • Because of the great size of the Achaemenid Empire and its frequent diplomatic contact with its subject nations, the Persians created a large number of public proclamations and biscripts associating Old Persian with Egyptian, Akkadian, Elamite, and even Greek.

Grotefend's Methodology
- • Numerous carved columns depicting the Achaemenid kings still stand in the ruins of Persepolis, and many of them bear short cuneiform inscriptions, which Grotefend presumed served as captions for the royal portraits. He compared these texts to copies of inscriptions made by Niebuhr at the site of Naqsh-e Rostam and was struck by the patterns he saw.

- • A comparison of two columns at Persepolis reveals that the Old Persian texts have slightly different styles. They're undoubtedly the same writing system, but they were made at different times and found in different wings of the palace. The "punctuation" sign noted by Niebuhr proved useful to Grotefend, allowing him to compare numerous inscriptions to look for common words, even without knowing whether the signs were alphabetic or syllabic.

- In patterns of word repetition in the different inscriptions, Grotefend found indications of a shared structure. This structural duplication suggested that the inscriptions were formulaic, with minimal variation. Given the Persian rhetoric recorded by Herodotus and present in the Greek biscripts at Naqsh-e Rostam, Grotefend surmised that some of the repeating elements in these inscriptions might provide the words for *king*, *great king*, and *son*, and the variable elements might provide the names of the depicted kings and their predecessors.

- Again, looking at patterns of repetition, Grotefend reasoned that some of the unidentified first words in the inscriptions might provide the name of a king, after which his titles would be assigned in a formulaic manner. The name of the king's father might be provided in the unidentified middle portion of the inscriptions.

- Grotefend decided to test his theory using the names of the non-royal Hystaspes; his son, King Darius I; and his grandson, King Xerxes I. He equated these names with possible pronunciations in Old Persian (Hytaspes = Vishtāspa, Darius = Dārayavahaush, and Xerxes = Xshayārshā) and noted shared phonetic signs in the inscriptions (**sh**, **a**, **r**, and **y**) corresponding to the pronunciations he had posited.

- Grotefend's findings were enough to rule out coincidence. Nonetheless, as we know today, he was only partly right. He thought that Old Persian was alphabetic, but it was a syllabary. Each of the signs Grotefend identified was actually a pronounceable syllable, carrying the values of consonant + vowel (or vowel alone).

- Using the values he had generated from the name of Xerxes, Grotefend was able to read the first four signs of a frequently repeated word in the inscriptions as **kh-sh-a-y**, which he linked with the Avestan word *khscheio*, meaning "chief, ruler." The connection to the repeating word for "king" in the speeches of Xerxes and the Naqsh-e Rostam inscriptions seemed clear.

- Grotefend was able to the read the inscription on one column as follows: "Xerxes, the great king, the king of kings, the son of Darius the king, an Achaemenian." Other column inscriptions at Persepolis are similar.

Other Achaemenid Biscripts
- The Achaemenids left behind many biscripts and bilingual inscriptions; perhaps the most fascinating biscripts are the ones that relate Old Persian, Elamite, and Babylonian to the language and writing of the ancient Egyptians.

- For example, a statue of Darius the Great was carved in Egypt in the late 6th century B.C. and sent to the Persian capital, where it was discovered by archaeologists in the early 1970s. On the robe and pedestal of the statue were inscriptions in four ancient scripts, providing the name of Darius I and his customary "king of kings" epithet.

- Equally noteworthy is an alabaster vase that came to light in Egypt in the late 18th century. It was described by the French archaeologist Caylus, but it wasn't until after Champollion's decipherment of Egyptian in 1822 that the vase could be recognized as having been dedicated to Xerxes I.
  - Some years later, as Grotefend's work became more widely known, the true value of the vase was finally recognized.

  - It's hard to imagine a more eloquent defense of the correctness of Champollion's and Grotefend's decipherments than that both of them managed to independently discover the name of Xerxes on the Caylus vase.

Suggested Reading

Booth, *The Discovery and Decipherment of the Trilingual Cuneiform Inscriptions.*

Kent, *Old Persian.*

Niebuhr, *Reisebeschreibung nach Arabien und andern umliegenden Ländern* (*Description of a Voyage to Arabia and the Neighboring Lands*).

Rawlinson, "The Persian Cuneiform Inscription at Behistun."

Questions to Consider

1. What is meant by the term *cuneiform*? You will now begin to notice (if you haven't already) a routine popular misuse of this word as implying that all cuneiform scripts are genetically related or even the same. Sometimes, the word is even equated with a language, as in "Do you speak cuneiform?" Where do you suppose this confusion comes from? How would you set someone straight about the proper use of this term?

2. What do you think about the preoccupation of the Achaemenid kings with status and genealogy in their inscriptions? Are these radically different from our own concerns, 2,500 years later? Why or why not?

What Does Cuneiform Say?
Lecture 16

In the modern province of Kermānshāh, Iran, visitors can still see a great low-relief sculpture of Darius I that was carved into Mount Behistun in about 500 B.C. As with the Achaemenid texts of Persepolis, the carved figures here are surrounded by cuneiform captions and more than 1,000 lines of text in Old Persian script, Elamite cuneiform, and Babylonian cuneiform. The main message of the Behistun monument is the legitimation and aggrandizement of Darius's rule, but we are lucky to have this bombastic ancient monument. Behistun was the final key to the decipherment of Old Persian and opened the door to the decipherment of Babylonian, Elamite, and earlier cuneiform scripts.

Deciphering Elamite

- As we saw in the last lecture, Grotefend had made a start on deciphering Old Persian by 1802, but he still regarded it as an alphabet. It wasn't until the Old Persian text of the Behistun cliff carving was finally published in 1846 that there was sufficient evidence to overturn the alphabet hypothesis in favor of a syllabary.

- The remarkable task of recording and analyzing the Old Persian text of the Behistun cliff carving was almost entirely the work of one man, the Englishman Henry Rawlinson (1810–1895). It took him 10 years to do the work, crawling and climbing over the sheer cliff face at great risk to life and limb.

- The lengthy Old Persian text and many shorter captions at Behistun contained the names of all the most important people of Darius's day. Comparing these names with their forms in Herodotus's *Histories* allowed Rawlinson to greatly improve the sign values first proposed by Grotefend. Further, because Old Persian was part of the Indo-European family tree, scholars at last had a strong knowledge of at least one of the three scripts and languages on the Behistun trilingual.

- Next, work began on the Elamite and Babylonian texts at Behistun. These were copied by Rawlinson during the 1840s and proved even more difficult than the Old Persian.
  - The 593 lines of Elamite were the first to be studied, and it was immediately apparent that this was a somewhat more complicated script than Old Persian, with 123 different signs. It was bound to be a syllabary, though it did have a few logographs for common words, such as *king* and *land*.

  - By comparing proper names in the Old Persian captions to parallel portions of the Elamite captions, the sound values of many of these signs could be worked out, and most of them were known by 1855.

  - Unfortunately, no sooner were these values tried out on the rest of the Elamite text than it became apparent that the language resembled no other, living or dead. Elamite is what linguists call an ***isolate***—a language with no known relatives. This has greatly hindered all additional work on this writing system.

- Although we can't unlock the Elamite language, the Elamite decipherment was still important. It revealed that the origin of Elamite cuneiform was the same Sumerian cuneiform that gave rise to Akkadian, Assyrian, and Babylonian, with many signs of shared shape and meaning.

Deciphering Babylonian
- The 112 lines of Babylonian were immediately more interesting than the Elamite inscription in that they could be related to numerous tablets that had made their way from Babylon to European museums in the preceding decades. The Babylonian script was much more complicated than either Old Persian or Elamite, with more than 600 signs. Such numbers indicate that Babylonian was a mixed script, with both logographs and phonetic syllables.

- As with the Elamite script, the sound values of Babylonian began to be worked out by comparing the proper names of the Old Persian captions to parallel portions of the Babylonian captions. However, given the complexity of the script and the radically different sounds involved, this was a fairly tricky process. Numerous other biscripts (from Persepolis, Naqsh-e Rostam, and excavations in Mesopotamia) were all needed to test equivalences.

- Luckily, it quickly became apparent that Babylonian was a Semitic language, related to Arabic, Hebrew, Aramaic, and Phoenician, among others.
  - This connection became clear when the new syllables (with unique phonetic signs, uncommon in most scripts) started consistently spelling known Semitic roots and words, such as **'il** ("god"), **mlk** ("king"), and so forth.

  - This discovery meant that peculiarities of sound and meaning could begin to be explained by comparison with other Semitic languages; the Babylonian inscriptions immediately became many times more intelligible than Elamite.

- In addition to Rawlinson, two other scholars began working on this problem: Edward Hincks (1792–1866) and Jules Oppert (1825–1905). Hincks is now credited with deducing much of the structure of this complex logosyllabic script, though his insights certainly rested on Rawlinson's careful copies of the inscriptions at Behistun.

Comparing Old Persian and Babylonian

- A comparison of Darius's doorway inscription from Persepolis with its Babylonian equivalent reveals how different the two scripts look, despite the fact that they're both cuneiform. Both texts basically say the same thing: "Darius, the great king, king of kings, king of countries, son of Hystaspes, the Achaemenian, who built this palace."

- The Old Persian text looks longer because every word had to be spelled out syllabically, whereas in the Babylonian text, many words could be spelled out with logograms. For instance, note the repetition of the group **xa-sha-a-ya-tha-i-ya** to spell *king*, compared to the repeating logograph meaning the same thing in the Babylonian inscription.

- The opening signs of each inscription spell Darius's name, which was **da-a-ra-ya-va-u-sha** in Old Persian and **da-ri-ia-a-mush** in Babylonian.
    - Compare the cuneiform signs for **da** and **a** here. Apart from both being wedge shaped, they look nothing alike. The reason for the dissimilarity is that these two writing systems are not historically related.

    - In contrast, if we were comparing Elamite and Babylonian, we would find several signs of similar shape and meaning, because both of these scripts trace their origins to early Akkadian, which was borrowed from Sumerian.

Tracing Cuneiform Borrowing
- If we trace Babylonian backward about 100 years from these inscriptions, we note an interesting feature of these cuneiform scripts: semantic signs.
    - According to the Bible, Nebuchadnezzar II captured and destroyed Jerusalem in 586 B.C. and deported many Israelites. But according to a brick inscription dedicated by Nebuchadnezzar during an expansion of Babylon's temples, he was nonetheless a deeply pious man and a great patron of his god Marduk.

    - The star-shaped sign at the beginning of this brick inscription comes from the Sumerian script, where it has the semantic value **DINGIR** (meaning both "god" and "sky"), as well as the phonetic value **an**. In Akkadian, the sign continued to be used as a semantic sign for "god" but could also be read **'il**, from the Semitic root that also meant "god."

    - In this brick text, the star-shaped sign qualifies the following sign, **NABU**, as the name of a Babylonian god. This sign is the first part of Nebuchadnezzar's name, which runs for five more blocks, halting at the Sumerian logograph **LUGAL** ("king").

○ The last four signs are also Sumerian but carry the Semitic reading *Bab'ili*. The final sign is a semantic one indicating that this is a place, namely, the city of Babylon. Together, the first line reads "Nebuchadnezzar, king of Babylon."

- If we go back 15 more centuries, to the Sumerian origins of this script, we note the visual complexity of the earlier cuneiform and the arrangement of the signs in rectangular boxes, rather than the linear arrangement we've seen among later scripts.

Earliest Mesopotamian Writing
- At the end of the 4th millennium B.C., Mesopotamian writing was highly pictorial, just like the earliest attested phases of Chinese characters and Egyptian hieroglyphs. Also like Chinese—but unlike Egyptian—Mesopotamian writing lost this highly pictorial quality and became more rectilinear and visually simplified through time.

Drawings and photographs of ancient inscriptions by Dr. Marc Zender, Tulane University.

The dedicatory inscription of Ur-Nammu reads, "For Inanna, his lady, Ur-Nammu, the mighty man, king of Ur, king of Sumer and Akkad, has built her temple."

- The first step in this process was probably the transfer of the script from a perishable medium, such as ink on papyrus, to the comparatively more durable but also clumsier medium of wax or clay. As with Chinese, a painted format would seem to be responsible for the flowing, curvilinear forms of these early pictographs, whereas the transfer to clay or wax would have promoted more angular forms and the technique of impression rather than incision.

- Scholars are divided about what precisely led to the next step, a 90-degree counterclockwise rotation of signs. Whatever the reason, the reorientation undoubtedly assisted the process of schematization as scribes began to lose track of the original pictorial motivation of signs.

- The third step involved making the sign by impressing reeds in a wax or clay surface rather than dragging the stylus through wet clay to make an incision. At this stage, major simplifications of the signs often took place, and these simplifications each developed in their own ways in various descendant scripts.

Influence of Cuneiform Literature
- The great library of Ashurbanipal (r. 669–631 B.C.) was discovered by Austen Henry Layard in 1849. This king and his successors had combed all of Asia to collect and copy a library of more than 10,000 cuneiform tablets in their palace at Nineveh. The tablets recorded myths, legends, scientific and geographical information, even the world's first map. The library also contained *The Epic of Gilgamesh*, a widely known story that had a resounding influence on later literature, including the Hebrew Bible.

- The influence of early cuneiform authors is even more widely felt in religious ordinances and law. Thus, the 3,000-year-old law code of Hammurabi is immediately recognizable as the ultimate source of several biblical laws, as well as the inspiration for the secular legislation of later eras.

- Ancient Mesopotamian scribes have bequeathed us a wide and varied literature. The contents of these cuneiform scripts are revelatory in many ways. Not only are they sometimes eerily modern—leading us to recognize our common humanity with individuals who lived in a very different time and place—but they also shine a light on the origins of practices and beliefs that continue to the present day.

Important Term

isolate: A language with no known relatives.

Suggested Reading

Adkins, *Empires of the Plain.*

Chiera, *They Wrote on Clay.*

Hincks, "On the Three Kinds of Persepolitan Writing and on the Babylonian Lapidary Characters."

Robinson, *The Story of Writing.*

Walker, *Cuneiform.*

Questions to Consider

1. What are the implications of the parallels between Utnapishtim's flood and Hammurabi's Code, as recorded in early cuneiform tablets, and Noah's flood and the Ten Commandments, as recorded in the Old Testament? How do these parallels help biblical scholars, archaeologists, and historians contextualize the early books of the Bible?

2. What do you think about the preoccupation of Ur-Nammu with the building of a temple for the goddess Inanna? Is this radically different from our own concerns 4,000 years later? Why or why not?

Mycenaean Linear B—An Aegean Syllabary

Lecture 17

In 1628 B.C., the Aegean island of Santoríni exploded in a cataclysmic volcanic eruption that spawned a massive tsunami. Ships and coastal settlements throughout the Aegean Sea were devastated, including the city of Knossos on the nearby island of Crete, once the center of a powerful trading empire. After the catastrophe in 1628, the wealthy citizens of Knossos (known as Minoans) were apparently weakened and were eventually overwhelmed by the Mycenaeans. These new arrivals adopted and adapted the Minoan writing system—an undeciphered script called Linear A—developing the complex script called Linear B. In this lecture, we'll discuss the discovery, decipherment, and contents of this intriguing ancient writing system.

Linear B and the Five Pillars

- The story of Cretan writing begins with the excavations of Sir Arthur Evans (1851–1941) at Knossos in 1900. For five years, he labored to uncover what he called the Palace of Minos, the seat of a Late Bronze Age kingdom. Evans unearthed the remains of at least three different writing systems spanning about 1,000 years, from 2200–1200 B.C.

- The earliest of these systems (2200–1700 B.C.) is an undeciphered hieroglyphic script. The second (1800–1450 B.C.) was a logosyllabic script named Linear Script A by Evans. This also remains undeciphered, although some scholars have suggested that Linear A may record a Semitic script allied with Phoenician or, perhaps, a language related to Lycian. The third script (1450–1200 B.C.) was named Linear Script B by Evans and is the only one of the three that has been deciphered.

- Linear B has about 210 signs in total; it is a syllabary with many semantic signs.

- We now know that at least 87 of its signs are phonetic syllables, giving either the five pure vowels (**a**, **e**, **i**, **o**, **u**) or consonant-vowel combinations (**pa**, **pe**, **pi**, and so on). The syllabary accounts for more than 90 percent of all the sign occurrences in the corpus.

- In addition to the syllables, there are 4 numerical signs, 1 word divider, and about 125 semantic signs. The role of these semantic signs is to reduce the ambiguity of phonetic spellings.

- There is a fairly ample corpus of Linear B texts, totaling about 6,000 tablets of various lengths.

- The language of Linear B is well known, though it took Michael Ventris's decipherment to reveal what it was: an archaic stage of Greek. It can be reconstructed by careful comparison of the many ancient and modern Greek dialects, as well as our understanding of the Indo-European family of languages, of which Greek is a member.

- Thanks largely to Homer, the cultural context of the Bronze Age Mycenaeans is fairly well known, including the names of people and places on Crete. Both Homer and Herodotus gave us place names that were critical to the decipherment of Linear B.

- The one great missing piece in Linear B has been a bilingual. Despite Ventris's eventual decipherment, the lack of a Linear B biscript is still keenly felt. There remains a fair degree of uncertainty about many phonetic and semantic signs, which has impeded scholars in moving beyond the obvious relationship between Linear B and Linear A to decipher the earlier script.

Evans's Attempt at Decipherment

- Evans first established the left-to-right reading order of Linear B. He also identified the word divider, which helped him to recognize that the pictorially derived semantic signs and the number signs appeared at the ends of words. He fairly quickly worked out the four numerical signs and was able to show that two particular signs probably spelled a word meaning "total."

- Another of Evans's breakthroughs was the identification of many of the semantic signs in Linear B. These were pictorial in origin, of course, so the images are fairly transparent. One fragmentary tablet from Pylos depicts six horses, some with manes and some without. It seemed reasonable to Evans to conclude that different kinds of horses were being counted on this tablet. Several of the horses were also qualified with phonetic signs.

  o Evans's interest in early Mediterranean scripts led him to recognize that the syllabic signs were from the Cypriotic syllabary. Cypriotic is related to Linear A and Linear B, though it was invented much later (800–250 B.C.). It has 54 signs, and it has several bilinguals with both Phoenician and the Greek alphabet. For this reason, it was easily deciphered, in 1871, and was clearly used to write a dialect of ancient Greek.

  o Cypriotic was also in use at the same time as the Greek alphabet, though it apparently had a longer history, as numerous shared signs between Linear B and Linear A suggest. It now seems clear that there was some historical connection among these three scripts, although the exact nature of that connection will have to await the decipherment of Linear A and more archaeological discoveries.

  o Evans saw that if he assumed that the two signs in front of the horse on the Pylos tablet had the same values as their lookalike signs in Cypriotic, they could be read **po-lo**, and *pōlō* was an early Greek word meaning "foal"! Had Evans followed this lead, he could well have deciphered Linear B, but he did not believe that Linear B was written in Greek.

The Work of Alice Kober (1907–1950)

- The American archaeologist Alice Kober made significant contributions to Linear B studies in the mid- to late 1940s. She noticed several groups of frequently repeated words from the Cretan tablets whose contexts suggested that they were place names, such as Knossos. She also noticed that these words turned up in various forms with systematic variation in their final signs. She interpreted these as *case endings*.

- Kober didn't commit to these (or any) specific meanings, but if she was right, then the case endings should be shared, which would enable inferences to be made about shared consonants or vowels between different signs. She constructed a tentative "grid" of signs that probably shared a vowel of the case suffix, along with others that probably shared the final consonant of one of the place names.

- Kober also noticed that the spellings of the common word for "total" varied depending on whether male or female objects were being counted. This suggested *gender marking* typical of Indo-European languages, such as Greek.

The Work of Michael Ventris

- Michael Ventris justly receives credit for demonstrating that Linear B recorded an early version of Greek, although his work rests on the foundations provided by Kober. He was able to extend Kober's grid, eventually drawing many of the syllabic signs into an intricate web of signs sharing consonants or vowels.

- Ventris noticed that there were five signs that appeared almost exclusively at the beginning of words in Linear B, and he reasonably assumed these to be the vowels **a, e, i, o,** and **u**. In a syllabic script, such as Linear B, the vowels in the middle and at the end of words are supplied by consonant-vowel signs, such as **po** and **lo**, but vowels at the beginning of words had to be written with vowel-only signs, such as **o**. This provided yet another script-internal check on decipherment.

- Because no bilingual was available, Ventris focused his efforts on the five Cretan place names identified by Kober. He noticed that three of them ended with the same sign, while two others shared a different final sign. But, on the basis of the declensions, both of these signs had to share the same vowel. Ventris suspected that the vowel was probably **-o**, given sign similarities with Cypriotic.

a mi ni so

ko no so

tu li so

pa i to

lu ki to

Drawings and photographs of ancient inscriptions by Dr. Marc Zender, Tulane University.

○ The three signs making up the second place name also shared this vowel. In other words, all three signs provided consonant **-o** sounds. This already suggested that it might provide the word *Knossos*, perhaps just **ko-no-so**, with the final *-s* unwritten.

○ Ventris also noted that the first sign of the first word was one of his vowel-only signs, and this sign shared the same vowel as the first sign of the fourth word. The sign looked exactly like Cypriotic **pa**. If it shared the vowel of the pure-vowel sign that began the first word, then that sign should be **a**.

○ This suggested that the first word might be **a-mi-ni-so** for *Amnisos* and the fourth word might be **pa-i-to** for *Phaistos*.

Kober had noticed several groups of frequently repeated words that might be place names; Ventris, in his efforts, focused on five particular names identified by Kober.

- Ventris was encouraged by the intersection of the internally derived grid, the place names, and the Cypriotic values. He tested his hypotheses in other contexts, found that they made sense, and published his results in July of 1952. The following year, the archaeologist Carl Blegen announced his discovery at Pylos of a tablet that provided several spellings further verifying Ventris's work.

Conclusions on Linear B

- Why would a script for Greek be so phonetically imprecise? The script was borrowed from speakers of an earlier Aegean language, which probably explains why it wasn't well adapted to Greek sounds. If we also factor in the resistance to change that all scripts share, as well as the relatively short time span in which Linear B was used, we can understand that there simply wasn't time for Linear B to develop more of the phonetic frills of the Greek language.

- The Greek language was represented by at least three different scripts in antiquity.
    - From 1450 to 1200 B.C., it was written in Linear B, which then vanished during the Greek dark ages. Four hundred years later, a related syllabic script reemerged on Cyprus, while still other speakers of Greek adopted and adapted the Phoenician alphabet.

    - Eventually, that Greek alphabet overwhelmed the Cypriotic syllabary. This is one of the many reasons that scholars assert that writing and language are not isomorphic. Any language can be served by multiple writing systems, and a single writing system, such as the Roman alphabet, can be used to write many unrelated languages.

- The decipherment of Linear B also punctured myths about ancient Aegean civilization. Before the writings could be read, scholars predicted they would discuss mythical topics, such as minotaurs and labyrinths; perhaps they even contained the earliest drafts of the works of Homer. Instead, the texts are focused on accounting: shipments of sheep and payments to tradesmen.

- Although the contents of Linear B texts are fairly boring, they still speak volumes about what was considered important in the ancient Aegean world. Following our theme of writing and civilization, this shows us once again just how adaptable writing is. This was Europe's earliest writing system, and it's intriguing to observe that our modern cultural fixation with property ownership, labor, and identity is apparently nothing new. Europeans have been paying taxes and asking for receipts for the last 3,500 years.

Important Terms

case ending: An inflectional ending on a noun, adjective, or pronoun that expresses the semantic relationship of the word to other words in the sentence. Typical cases include accusative (direct object), dative (indirect object), and genitive (possession or close association).

gender marking: System by which nouns in a language carry special endings or require distinctive pronoun, adjective, and article forms. In Indo-European languages, the genders are often masculine, feminine, and neuter. For example: German *der Löffel* ("the spoon"), *die Gabel* ("the fork"), and *das Messer* ("the knife").

Suggested Reading

Chadwick, *The Decipherment of Linear B*.

———, *Linear B and Related Scripts*.

Doumas, *Thera: Pompeii of the Ancient Aegean*.

Fox, "Alice E. Kober, 43; Lost to History No More."

Homer, *The Iliad*.

———, *The Odyssey*.

Kober, "Inflection in Linear Class B: 1—Declension."

———, "The Minoan Scripts."

———, "'Total' in Minoan (Linear Class B)."

Marinatos, "The Volcanic Destruction of Minoan Crete."

Pellegrino, *Unearthing Atlantis*.

Robinson, *The Man Who Deciphered Linear B*.

———, *The Story of Writing*.

Ventris, "King Nestor's Four-Handled Cups."

————, "Work Notes on Minoan Language Research and Other Unedited Papers."

Ventris and Chadwick, "Evidence for Greek Dialect in the Mycenaean Archives."

————, *Documents in Mycenaean Greek*.

Questions to Consider

1. What do you think of Evans's argument that Linear B could not possibly record the Greek language because both the Cypriotic syllabary and the Greek alphabet were already used for this purpose? What other languages have (or have had) multiple different writing systems? Why do you suppose this happens? And what does it tell us about the nature of the relationship between language and writing?

2. What do you think about the preoccupation of the Mycenaeans with temple accounts and taxation in their Linear B tablets? Is this radically different from our own concerns, 3,500 years later? Why or why not?

Mayan Glyphs—A New World Logosyllabary
Lecture 18

Yuri Knorosov was a Ukrainian-born, Soviet-educated linguist. Before World War II, he had studied Egyptology at Moscow State University. After the war, he also studied Chinese and Japanese before turning to Mayan hieroglyphs. Western scholars at the time, particularly the English anthropologist Sir J. Eric S. Thompson, believed that Mayan hieroglyphs were ideographic, but Knorosov's isolation in the Soviet Union and his lack of contact with other Mayanists protected him from the ideographic fallacy. In this lecture, we'll look at Mayan writing from the perspective of the five pillars of decipherment and follow the methodology of Knorosov that allowed him to overturn the mistaken ideas of the West.

Reception of Knorosov's Decipherment

- Yuri Knorosov began his decipherment of Mayan hieroglyphic writing around the same time that Michael Ventris revealed his discovery that Linear B inscriptions recorded ancient Greek. Working in Leningrad, Knorosov faced obstacles not encountered by his Western contemporaries. He was effectively cut off from the American and European schools that had long served as the traditional centers of Maya studies. Interestingly, Knorosov's isolation behind the Iron Curtain would both help and hinder his decipherment.

- Adequate dictionaries and grammars of Mayan languages were scarce in the 1950s, and several key sources, as well as records of Mayan inscriptions, were unavailable in Russia.
  - For these reasons, Knorosov restricted himself in his early work to the Yucatec Mayan language, spoken in the northern Yucatán Peninsula of Mexico and northern Belize and well documented since the colonial era.

  - Knorosov also restricted his decipherment to the three surviving Maya codices, screenfold books of the 13th–15th centuries, that had made their way into European collections in Madrid, Paris, and Dresden during the 16th century.

- Knorosov's decipherment had to overcome shortfalls in two of our pillars: language and corpus. In the end, his decipherment was somewhat limited and contained several errors. But other scholars would apply Knorosov's methods to earlier stone inscriptions and trace the development of Mayan writing over almost 2,000 years.

- Knorosov's findings, published in 1952, were not well received by Western scholars. Dr. Gordon Ekholm, associate director of anthropology at the Museum of Natural History, responded to the news of Knorosov's decipherment by saying, "Mayan hieroglyphics is a form of picture writing, each symbol of which is believed to represent an entire phrase or idea rather than a single letter or word." It took more than a decade for Knorosov's views to begin to be accepted in the West.

The Five Pillars and Mayan Writing
- The strength of our current decipherment of Mayan writing, which can now be counted among the most successful and complete of all decipherments, is directly owed to the solid foundation provided by the five pillars of decipherment.

- First, the type of script is known and was quickly divined by Knorosov. Mayan writing uses more than 500 signs, strongly suggesting a mixed script, probably a syllabary with logographs and/or semantic signs.
  - We now know that Mayan writing was in use from about 400 B.C. to A.D. 1600. Coupled with the large area over which Mayan writing was used, including the modern countries of Mexico, Guatemala, Belize, and Honduras, it's easy to guess that the system must have changed over time and that it probably involved a certain degree of regional variation.

o At present count, scholars have cataloged more than 2,000 different Mayan signs. But no more than 500 or so were in use at any given time; thus, Knorosov was right to use that figure.

o About 100 of these signs are phonetic syllables, either giving the five pure vowels (**a**, **e**, **i**, **o**, **u**) only or consonant-vowel combinations (such as **ka**, **ke**, **ki**, and so on). These signs are used to spell out Mayan words or to provide phonetic complements, derivations, or inflections for Mayan logograms.

o In addition to the syllabic signs, there are about 400 logograms. Intriguingly, Mayan writing does not include semantic signs. Based on current evidence, there is no parallel in New World writing systems for the kinds of semantic signs seen in Old World scripts.

• Second, there is a large corpus of Mayan texts. Thousands of inscriptions are known in a diversity of media, including books; murals; ceramics; monumental inscriptions; and scores of portable inscriptions in stone, shell, and bone. The subject matter of Mayan inscriptions is equally varied, with such genres as folktales, mythology, religious ritual, and political history. Several programs of publication ensure the rapid dissemination of most new discoveries.

• Third, the language of Mayan hieroglyphic writing is now well known, and even before Knorosov, it should have been obvious that it was an early form of Mayan, given that Mayan languages continue to be spoken in and around the ancient cities where the hieroglyphs were carved. Although half a dozen of these languages have become extinct in the modern era and still others are endangered, there were once at least 37 distinct Mayan languages spoken in this area.

o The comparison of these 37 Mayan languages has allowed linguists to work out much of the Mayan family tree and a fairly detailed reconstruction of Proto-Mayan, the ancestor of the whole family, probably last spoken thousands of years ago in the Cuchumatanes mountain range of western Guatemala.

- o Recall that the Egyptian language was first recorded more than 5,000 years ago, and Coptic is its only surviving descendant. By contrast, we are much closer in time to the beginning of Mayan writing (currently placed no more than 2,500 years ago), and there are 37 related languages, including 8 languages that are very closely related, at least 2 of which are direct descendants. Thus, the linguistic decipherment of Mayan writing is on a much more solid footing than Egyptian.

- Fourth, thanks largely to the efforts of early Franciscan missionaries, the cultural context of the Maya was reasonably well known even in Knorosov's day, including the names of several historical figures, gods, and places.
  - o Even more important was a list of the names of the Maya days and months in their ancient calendar, which recur with remarkable frequency in nearly all of the inscriptions.

  - o There is also a certain amount of cultural continuity among the numerous groups of speakers of Mayan languages today, meaning that ethnographic and linguistic fieldwork continues to yield new insights into earlier Maya culture.

- Finally, Mayan decipherment has been blessed with a number of useful biscripts. By far the most important of these come from Diego de Landa's *Relacíon de las cosas de Yucatán*, or "*Account of the Things of Yucatán*." Written in the mid-16th century but lost until the late 19th century, this work provided an invaluable survey of Maya culture and history, including many details of cultural context.
  - o In his book, Landa attempted to relate 27 Mayan signs to the Spanish alphabet—clearly working from the incorrect assumption that Mayan writing was an alphabet. Any effort to apply this alphabet straightforwardly to ancient Mayan inscriptions is doomed to failure, but it was still an honest

attempt to elicit the workings of Mayan hieroglyphs from a knowledgeable informant.

○ In addition to the more famous "alphabet," Landa also included glyphs for the 18 named months of the Maya calendar. These are not only glossed by Landa with their names in Yucatec Mayan, but they are composed of 53 individual signs (a combination of syllables and logograms) whose values we comprehend today and can make sense of in these contexts. The 20 named days of the Maya calendar are also given in glyphic and alphabetic form.

○ Finally, Landa provided two isolated words written glyphically (*noose* and *water*) and the glyphic sentence *I don't want to*.

Knorosov's Approach

- Knorosov began his decipherment by looking at the 27 signs given alphabetic values in Landa's manuscript. He noticed that 3 signs were associated with the letter A, 2 with the letter B, 2 with L, and so on. Knorosov knew that ***allographs*** (signs of different shape with the same value) were a common feature of mixed logosyllabic scripts with hundreds of signs, but they were not typical of alphabets. Knorosov also knew from his study of the Mayan books that there were hundreds of signs in total, which also suggested that this was a mixed script of phonetic and word signs.

- Knorosov further noticed that most of the signs in Landa's list were associated with single letters, such as the signs for A and B, but some of the signs were associated with consonant-vowel combinations, including the signs **ca**, **cu**, **ku**, and **ti**. Knorosov believed that all of these signs might actually be syllables, even the ones glossed simply B, L, and so forth.

- Knorosov cemented this observation by noting Landa's own description of how he had elicited the alphabet from a knowledgeable Maya scribe.

- Landa makes it plain that he asked the scribe to spell out the Mayan words for "noose" and "water" by spelling out the words using Spanish letter names. In other words, instead of asking the scribe to write the word for "noose" (Mayan: *le'*), Landa asked for the letters using their Spanish names.

- Going back to Landa's "alphabet," Knorosov recognized that it must have been elicited in the same way. Today, we can explain all the signs in Landa's various biscripts, in light of both Knorosov's decipherment and his recognition of Landa's elicitation process.

- Knorosov realized that he needed to treat his own proposed sign values as hypotheses and test them in other contexts. He had access only to late Mayan books in European collections, but fortunately, these were much closer to Landa's time than any of the earlier stone inscriptions. Working with the Madrid Codex and the Dresden Codex, Knorosov deciphered glyph blocks for *turkey*, *dog*, and *eleven* and verified his findings in Yucatec dictionaries.

- Knorosov's method was productive because it stripped away the poetic, metaphorical, and ideographic explanations that had dominated the study of Mayan writing before he came along, and because it could be constantly tested against new contexts. Either these tests would generate sensible readings in context or something was amiss and the values would have to be revisited as a result. The method was self-correcting.

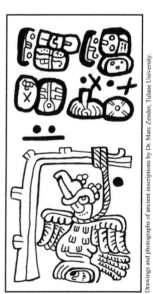

Drawings and photographs of ancient inscriptions by Dr. Marc Zender, Tulane University.

Knorosov began his decipherment with a well-known page of the Madrid Codex, in which a glyph block referring to *turkey* could be isolated.

- The power of Knorosov's methodology is attested by the fact that of the 20 glyphic readings he presented in his 1952 paper, all but 1 continues to be accepted more than 60 years later. But the story of Mayan decipherment is hardly over. Knorosov had focused exclusively on phonetic signs, and he had looked at only the last 300 years of Mayan writing. Hundreds of undeciphered word signs and more than 1,700 years of earlier Mayan writing remained to be deciphered.

Important Term

allograph: Refers to the relationship between two or more graphically distinct signs that carry identical reading values. From a synchronic perspective, allographs are signs that are freely interchangeable. From a diachronic perspective, such signs are often the result of either sound change (where signs of different origin come to convey the same sound) or graphic divergence (where a sign takes on two different forms over time).

Suggested Reading

Coe, *Breaking the Maya Code.*

Pope, *The Story of Decipherment.*

Robinson, *The Story of Writing.*

Questions to Consider

1. What were the differences in the backgrounds of Thompson and Knorosov that allowed the latter to decipher Mayan hieroglyphic writing? Are there more general lessons to be drawn from these differences? If so, what are they?

2. Compare and contrast Thompson's and Knorosov's explanations of the hieroglyphic compounds for the words *turkey*, *dog*, and *eleven*. Which do you find most convincing and why? What was Thompson's main weakness as an epigrapher?

What Do the Mayan Glyphs Say?
Lecture 19

Mayan writing seems uncannily similar to Egyptian hieroglyphs. Both of these writing systems are highly pictorial, both have phonetic signs and logographic signs, and both combine these signs in strikingly similar ways. But archaeologists have found no indication of contact between the Maya and the Egyptians, and their writing systems are actually only superficially similar; they have none of the shared sign shapes, sign values, and spelling practices that characterize related scripts. How, then, can we explain the strikingly similar structural features of these unrelated scripts? In this lecture, we'll explore the structure of Mayan writing and look at a few of the many examples of ancient Mayan writing available to scholars.

The Maya and Our Understanding of Writing

- The appearance of pictorial signs of phonetic and logographic type in unrelated scripts, along with the principle of phonetic complementation in these scripts, has led scholars to believe that these must be universal features of writing. That is, they arose because their users came up with the same solution for how to best represent language in a graphic medium.

- Through the decipherment of Mayan writing, scholars have also learned that semantic signs are not a universal feature of writing. These signs serve to reduce ambiguity and are required only in scripts where phonetic spellings leave room for ambiguity.
  - None of the three Egyptian scripts recorded vowels, producing many ambiguous contexts in which the reader needed some guidance about which vowels to insert. There were several possible responses to this ambiguity, including the invention of signs for vowels, but the Egyptians innovated semantic signs instead.

○ It makes sense that some scripts would solve this problem in another way, increasing phonetic representation rather than inventing semantic signs. This is exactly what we see in the history of the alphabet, including the Greek innovation of vowel signs. And like the Greek alphabet, Mayan hieroglyphic writing is remarkably phonetic, capturing almost all of the important phonemic distinctions of the language.

The Structure of Mayan Writing

- In the wake of Knorosov's decipherment, scholars have had remarkable success in deciphering the hundreds of logograms in Mayan writing. Part of the reason for this is that the same word could be written in several ways, and by paying close attention to these variations, scholars could discern how logograms and phonetic signs cooperated to spell different words in the system.

- Consider the word *bahlam*, meaning "jaguar." The most basic way to spell this word is with the logogram **BAHLAM**. It originated as a recognizable picture of a jaguar, but it isn't a pictograph; rather, it's a logogram that always cues the word *bahlam*.

- Mayan writing also has many syllabic signs, and a scribe could complement the **BAHLAM** logogram with a suffixed syllable **ma**, giving a phonetic clue that the word ended in *-m*. The presence or absence of redundant phonetic complements seems to have been based on the whim of the scribe. Because the **BAHLAM** sign never has any other reading, the presence of **-ma** can't be motivated by the reduction of ambiguity.

- Instead, it seems likely that the principle began to provide important information in the form of grammatical prefixes and suffixes.
  ○ To use an English example, we can convert the verb *bake* into the ***agentive noun*** *baker* by adding the suffix *-er*. Once this kind of practice became commonplace in Mayan, complementation was also adopted for rare logograms as an aid to comprehension. Only afterwards would it have spread by analogy throughout the system.

○ Whatever the origin of this practice, it's a remarkable boon to epigraphers. Because the **ma** syllable was provided in Landa's 16th-century list of Mayan signs, it was deciphered well before the "jaguar" sign was. Such spellings provided the first clue that *bahlam* was the value of the logogram.

- The final evidence for the *bahlam* value came from several contexts in which the scribes dispensed with the logogram altogether and simply wrote the word *bahlam* with the syllabic signs **ba**, **la**, and **ma**.

- You may have noted a discrepancy between the Mayan word for "jaguar," reconstructed by historical linguists as *bahlam*, and the phonetic spelling of this word in Mayan hieroglyphs as **ba-la-ma**. Namely, the /h/ in the middle of the word isn't written.
  - ○ In a writing system whose smallest phonetic building blocks were either vowels or consonant-vowel syllables, there was no way to record consonant clusters without oversupplying a vowel.

  - ○ As in Linear B, some important sounds, such as this internal /h/, are therefore consistently abbreviated in Mayan writing. Fortunately, we know enough about the 37 Mayan languages that we're able to reconstruct such things even when they're not recorded by the ancient writing system.

Mayan Allographs
- Another set of spellings nicely illustrates the frequent allographs in Mayan writing, that is, formally different signs that freely substitute with one another. For example, the word *pakal*, meaning "shield," can also be written in several ways.

- The logogram **PAKAL** depicts a hand shield of a type that is well known from Maya art. It's pictorial in origin, again, but it doesn't simply mean "shield" in a vague way; it always represents the word *pakal*, so its function is as a logogram. Like the jaguar glyph, it can receive the redundant phonetic complement **-la** underscoring its final *-l*.

- In addition to illustrating the frequency of allographs in Mayan writing, the differences in three syllabic spellings of *pakal* also nicely illustrate the idea that the pictorial nature of Mayan signs gives no clue as to their functions in the script. Just as we saw with Egyptian hieroglyphs, pictography is merely a process of sign formation, not a kind of sign.

The Contents of Mayan Writing
- Mayan writing is remarkably pervasive. It appears on both monumental and portable objects and in a great diversity of media, including paper, wood, stone, ceramics, textiles, shell, bone, and even human skin.

- This diversity of media suggests an equally diverse series of messages, and indeed, Mayan texts record the ownership of important objects, speak about personal ritual practices, recount humorous folktales and sacred mythology, and chronicle politically charged local and regional histories.

- An inscription found on the underside of a carved limestone lintel from the site of Yaxchilan in Chiapas, Mexico, represents the height of Maya sculptural achievement in the early 8th century. The carving depicts a highly personal scene of ritual activity.
  - The left figure is clearly a male, captured in midstride while he holds a burning spear. He is identified by the hieroglyphs above as the king Itzamnaaj Bahlam, who ruled Yaxchilan from A.D. 681 to 742. The hieroglyphs explain that the king's image is "in the act of penance with a fiery spear."

  - The king's wife, Lady K'abal Xook, kneels to the right and draws a thorn-studded rope through her tongue. Blood spatters her cheeks and falls into the basket of bloodletting implements and ritual books between them. The short text to the left identifies her and tells us that this is also "her image in the act of penance."

o Given the secrecy with which such rites were conducted, it's doubtful we would ever have understood their importance had Mayan glyphs not been deciphered.

- Another inscription is on a large, four-sided *altar* (Altar Q) from the site of Copan, Honduras. Each side depicts four individuals seated on their hieroglyphic names and titles, and the upper surface contains a historical text of 36 glyph-blocks in length. Thanks to the decipherment of Mayan, we know that these individuals were sequent kings of a dynasty that ruled Copan for more than 350 years.

Burnt offerings and the nourishing of the gods with human blood, as shown on the lintel from Yaxchilan, were sacred ritual activities and deeply personal sacraments.

o The west side of the monument depicts the dynastic founder, K'inich Yax K'uk' Mo', just left of the center. He is shown as a foreigner, holding a burning torch and square shield and wearing a circular eye ornament that associates him with the great western metropolis of Teotihuacan in central Mexico.

o He was succeeded by his son, depicted at far left, and 14 additional kings, culminating in the reign of Yax Pasaj Chan Yopaat, who is seated just right of center, as if in dialogue with his distant predecessor.

o Scholars were initially skeptical about the history related by this monument. However, archaeological excavations at

Copan during the past 30 years have uncovered the buildings, inscriptions, and mortal remains of most of the earlier kings depicted on Altar Q, and future excavations will undoubtedly discover the rest of them.

- Finally, we see a lengthy narrative scene from a Classic Maya vase. This object was excavated illicitly in the 1970s and sold on the international art market.
  - ○ The horizontal band of larger hieroglyphs just below the vessel's rim tells us that this was the chocolate drinking cup owned or commissioned by a late-7th-century king of Naranjo, K'ahk' Tiliw Chan Chahk.

  - ○ Also on the vase are two sequent narrative scenes, punctuated by hieroglyphic captions. These captions are actually attached to the mouths of the figures in these scenes and represent spoken words—like an ancient comic book! The vase depicts a humorous story of a rabbit who steals the clothing and jewelry of a rich merchant god.

- It's impossible to exaggerate the importance of the highly varied contents of Mayan writing for our understanding of ancient Maya civilization. Although there are still important linguistic and cultural links between the modern Maya and their ancestors, most of what we know about ancient Maya sociopolitical organization, humor, religion, and elite culture comes to us from the decipherment of Mayan hieroglyphic writing.

Important Terms

agentive noun: Denotes a person, animal, or thing that performs a specified action or activity (e.g., *worker, baker*). In English, agentive nouns can be derived from verbs by adding *-er*. In Mayan, this is done by adding *aj-* (e.g., *ajtz'ihb*, "writer, scribe").

altar: An offering table used in ceremonies.

Suggested Reading

Coe and Van Stone, *Reading the Maya Glyphs.*

McLuhan, *The Gutenberg Galaxy.*

Stone and Zender, *Reading Maya Art.*

Stuart, "Breaking the Code."

Zender, *Diacritical Marks and Underspelling in the Classic Maya Script.*

———, "*Baj* 'Hammer' and Related Affective Verbs in Classic Mayan."

Questions to Consider

1. Why isn't the fact that the Maya and the Egyptians both built pyramids relevant to arguments about contact between New and Old World civilizations before the Viking era? What evidence would anthropologists, archaeologists, linguists, and epigraphers need to seriously entertain the idea of transatlantic contact?

2. What do you think about the preoccupation of Itzamnaaj Bahlam and Lady K'abal Xook with their private devotions to the Yaxchilan patron god Aj K'ahk' O' Chahk? Is this radically different from our own concerns, roughly 1,300 years later? Why or why not?

Aztec Hieroglyphs—A Recent Decipherment
Lecture 20

A ztec writing owes very little to earlier writing systems in central Mexico. Its phonetic signs and logograms derive from Nahuatl, and the script appears to be an Aztec invention, designed to record the Nahuatl language. It seems to have been invented just 200 years before the arrival of the Spanish and continued to be used for more than 100 years after the conquest, disappearing in the mid-17th century. Despite its brief existence, Aztec hieroglyphic writing has much to teach us about the history and development of the Nahuatl language before the arrival of the Spanish, and its continued use during the first century of the colonial era sheds light on early interactions between Spaniards and Aztecs in New Spain.

Aztec Writing and the Five Pillars

- Aztec writing is clearly of the logosyllabic type. Although the script is still not completely deciphered, scholars have counted more than 400 logograms and around 50 phonetic signs, all of them either pure vowels or consonant-vowel combinations. These syllabic signs are used to spell out Nahuatl words or to provide phonetic complements to logograms. As with Mayan writing, the Aztec script does not appear to include semantic signs.

- The corpus of Aztec texts is not as large or diverse as scholars would like, but it has proven ample for the purposes of decipherment. Unfortunately, there are only a few dozen inscriptions in stone from the preconquest period, most of them rather short, and all of them providing dates in the Aztec calendar, place names, or the names of Aztec emperors.

- The language recorded by Aztec hieroglyphic writing is well known. As the lingua franca of the Aztec Empire, Classical Nahuatl was amply recorded in the colonial era, and we have excellent dictionaries, grammars, and texts documenting this language during the last 500 years. About a dozen modern regional dialects of the

Nahuatl language are still spoken today by more than 1 million modern Mexicans.

- o Nahuatl is a member of the large Uto-Aztecan language family, which stretches from Utah to Nicaragua. Combined, these languages allow us to reconstruct Proto-Uto-Aztecan with some confidence and to trace the development of the Nahuatl language over thousands of years.

- o Nahuatl has a written record longer than any other language in the New World apart from Mayan, stretching from the early 14th century to the present day.

- The cultural context of Aztec hieroglyphic writing is well known and detailed in numerous books by early missionaries. Of particular importance here is the Franciscan friar Bernardino de Sahagún, who compiled an encyclopedic Nahuatl-Spanish work on Aztec culture with the assistance of literate informants. Now known as the Florentine Codex, this work details Aztec calendrics, mythology, religion, and history.

- Finally, Aztec writing provides dozens of biscripts. Most Aztec texts come from the first 100 years of the Spanish colonial era and continued to be produced during this period, recording genealogies, histories, maps, and legal documents. In most of these documents, alphabetic glosses appear alongside the hieroglyphs, usually providing their reading in Nahuatl and occasionally providing an interpretative translation in Spanish or Latin.

Aztec Documents

- The Codex Mendoza was commissioned by the viceroy of New Spain around 1540 as a record of the conquests of the Aztec emperors and the tribute owed to them. The pages were laid out with ample blank space between pictorial scenes and hieroglyphs to accommodate neat Roman alphabetic glosses indicating the reading of hieroglyphic elements.

- o On one page, just left of center, an Aztec emperor is depicted seated on a reed throne and wearing a turquoise diadem. His name glyph floats behind his head, attached to the back of his robe by a short tether. This glyph is a compound of two signs: a logogram reading **TIS**, "chalk," and the phonetic sign **xo**. Together, these provide an abbreviated spelling for the name Tizoçicatzin, indicated in Roman letters on the emperor's cloak. Today, we usually call this emperor Tizoc.

○ The left side of the page references six years by their Aztec hieroglyphs, enclosed in square cartouches. Below them, in Spanish, is the alphabetic gloss "*numero de años*. 6," recording the number of years that Tizoc ruled (1481–1486).

○ Tizoc is depicted as speaking, and the hieroglyphs to the right record his speech as *mitl chimalli* (meaning "war"). He has declared war on the 14 city-states listed on the rest of the page, their hieroglyphic names all yoked to icons of burning and collapsing temples, indicating that they've been defeated.

- In other documents, the alphabetic glosses were clearly an afterthought, as revealed by the strange angles of the writing, worked in at some unknown time after the initial composition. A good example is the Matricula de Tributos, an early colonial register of tributes.

El Comandante /Wikimedia Commons/Public Domain.

The tribute items owed by city-states to the Aztec Empire are indicated pictorially on the Matricula de Tributos.

  ○ Here, a group of eight place names appears at the bottom of the page. The first is the logogram **WEWE**, pictorially derived from a portrait of an old man. This is an abbreviated spelling for Huehuetlan, a city in the Soconusco region of coastal Chiapas. Other place names are written with one or more logograms or with combinations of logograms and phonetic signs.

○ These eight city-states in the Soconusco region owed tribute to the capital of the Aztec Empire on a biennial basis. At the top left and right corners of the page are the glyphs for the Aztec months Ochpaniztli and Tlacaxipehualiztli, indicating when the tribute was due.

The Tyranny of the Gloss
- Ironically, the uniquely abundant biscripts for Aztec writing didn't lead to early decipherment but to a long tradition of studying the Roman alphabetic glosses alone, without much attention paid to the system underlying Aztec writing.
  ○ Even the glyphs on preconquest stone monuments, which don't include glosses, usually provide the same dates, rulers' names, and place names attested in colonial documents. Thus, these glyphs were usually compared *in toto*, with little concern for their individual parts.

  ○ As a result, a view of Aztec hieroglyphic writing as pictographic or ideographic has long dominated popular accounts.

- As an example, consider the Stone of Tizoc, discovered in the main square of Mexico City in the late 18th century. Around its circumference, the monument depicts the emperor Tizoc and several of his predecessors capturing the patron gods of 15 different ethnic groups.
  ○ Tizoc is named with the same hieroglyph as in the Codex Mendoza. The hieroglyphs of the 15 conquered groups could be reconciled with similar place names in the tribute documents, all interpreted on the basis of their glosses.

  ○ But the colonial-era glosses aren't always complete, as when the general label Xoconochco is used in the Matricula de

Tributos to refer to an entire region where eight distinct city-states were located.

o   In the Codex Mendoza, the sixth conquest of Tizoc's reign is identified in the alphabetic gloss as Toluca, a large region to the west of the Valley of Mexico. By contrast, the glyphs can be read as **MATLA-TZIN** and **TOLO-TEPE**, providing the abbreviated reference "the Matlatzincans of Tolucatepec." This refers to the conquest of a specific ethnic group dwelling in the mountains of Toluca. Despite the customary *abbreviation* of several predictable suffixes, the hieroglyphs are more specific than the gloss.

o   Importing this information back to the Stone of Tizoc, we can see that the emperor grasps the forelock of a captive god labeled with the hieroglyphic **MATLA**. This is an even more abbreviated spelling of Matlatzinca, referring to the ethnic group whose patron god this was. It's only by paying close attention to the details of the hieroglyphic spellings, rather than the glosses, that we can recover features that escaped the early colonial gloss-makers.

Decipherment of Aztec Writing

• Given the long concentration on glosses, it wasn't until the 19th century that scholars first began to consider Aztec writing on its own merits. The most important figure in this period was Joseph Marius Alexis Aubin (1802–1891), an independently wealthy Americanist and a collector of ancient Mexican manuscripts. With firsthand access to many primary sources, Aubin set out in 1830 to rigorously compare Aztec hieroglyphs to their glosses in dozens of documents.

• Aubin's observations were published in 1849 in a study titled *Notes on the Didactic Paintings and Figurative Writing of the Ancient Mexicans*. Not only did he note the clear and consistent distinction between narrative pictography ("didactic paintings") and Aztec hieroglyphs proper ("figurative writing"), but he also penetrated to the core of the writing system, recognizing that it contained both logograms and phonetic signs.

- Aubin's most important discovery was the substitution of logographic and phonetic spellings of the same name. Thus, in the Codex Vergara, he was able to show that the Nahuatl name Itzcoatl, "Obsidian serpent," was frequently written with the logograms **ITZ** ("obsidian") and **KOA** ("snake").

  ○ Because the signs are pictorial in origin, it's easy to see why many scholars regarded them as mere pictograms or ideograms, potentially readable in any language.

  ○ But Aubin showed that the "snake" part of the name was sometimes written with the phonetic signs **ko** and **a** instead, straightforwardly spelling out the word *koa*, "snake." As he noted, only phoneticism can explain this—not ideography or symbolism.

  ○ Aubin also recognized that the origins of the **ko** and **a** signs were acrophonic, stemming from the Nahuatl words *komitl* ("vase") and *atl* ("water"). Aubin went on to demonstrate that all of the phonetic syllables he could identify also had sources in the Nahuatl language, strongly suggesting that either the Aztecs or another Nahuatl-speaking group must have invented this writing system.

- One principle that eluded Aubin was phonetic complementation. This wasn't noted until 1888, when Zelia Maria Nuttall (1857–1933) published a perceptive short article entitled "On the Complementary Signs of the Mexican Graphic System." She had noted that certain Aztec signs redundantly repeated the initial or final sounds of logograms, providing a clue to their reading. In interpreting this feature of Aztec writing, Nuttall referenced Egyptian phonetic complements, perhaps the first instance of a comparative approach to the decipherment of a New World script.

- In 2008, the Spanish Mesoamericanist Alfonso Lacadena published two detailed studies of Aztec writing, following up on the insights of Aubin and Nuttall. He noted that Nuttall's principle of phonetic complementation was the key to identifying which signs were logograms and which were phonetic syllables. Applying this principle to both preconquest and postconquest sources, Lacadena and other scholars have been able to systematize and extend Aubin's decipherment.

- We have now deciphered at least 45 Aztec syllabic signs and at least 400 word signs, as well as abbreviational conventions eerily similar to those of Mycenaean Linear B. Given the impossibility of any historical connection between these two scripts, this provides another remarkable example of the universal features of logosyllabic writing systems.

Important Term

abbreviation: A conventional incomplete spelling of a word (e.g., English *Mr.* for *Mister*). Abbreviations can seem like errors, but they're usually systematic and codified. For instance, the Linear B, Mayan, and Aztec scripts routinely omit the spelling out of final consonants.

Suggested Reading

Aubin, *Mémoires sur la peinture didactique et l'écriture figurative des anciens.*

Lacadena, "Regional Scribal Traditions."

———, "A Nahuatl Syllabary."

Nicholson, "Phoneticism in the Late Pre-Hispanic Central Mexican Writing System."

Nuttall, "On the Complementary Signs of the Mexican Graphic System."

Townsend, *The Aztecs* (especially pp. 206–212).

Zender, "One Hundred and Fifty Years of Nahuatl Decipherment."

1. Given the profound structural similarities between Aztec and Mayan hieroglyphic writing, with their hundreds of logograms, phonetic syllables, and the principle of phonetic complementation, why do you suppose the Aztecs never wrote the lengthy texts that characterize earlier Mayan writing?

2. Some scholars have supposed that Aztec writing is restricted to names and calendrics so that it could be "read in any language." Is this position supported by what you've learned about Aztec writing? Why or why not?

3. What do you think about the preoccupation of the Aztec emperor Tizoc with presenting his victories on the field of battle? Is this radically different from our own concerns, a little more than 500 years later? Why or why not?

Etruscan and Meroïtic—Undeciphered Scripts
Lecture 21

Beginning with Champollion almost 200 years ago, epigraphers have had remarkable success in deciphering ancient scripts. Egypt, Mesopotamia, Crete, and Mexico have all given up their secrets. Scholars can now compare writing systems of all known types, around the world, and over more than 7,000 years of development. Universal features of writing systems, such as phonetic signs and phonetic complementation, have been discovered, as well as intriguing regional differences, such as the lack of semantic signs in the New World. But in this lecture, we turn to some of the failures of decipherment. Studying undeciphered scripts not only helps us better appreciate the limits of decipherment but, surprisingly, also sheds light on ancient civilizations.

Obstacles to Decipherment

- Despite decades of effort by many qualified epigraphers, dozens of scripts remain undeciphered. These include the Indus script of the Indus River valley of Pakistan, three early scripts of Crete, the Etruscan alphabet of northern Italy, the Meroïtic alphabet of the Sudan, and others. These systems remain undeciphered because they are lacking one or more of the five pillars, without which decipherment is always hindered if not impossible.

- None of the most well-known undeciphered scripts will be deciphered unless new information becomes available. Biscripts and underlying languages are needed for most of these scripts, and it's quite possible that such material doesn't exist. In those cases, the scripts may never be deciphered.

- The Etruscan and Meroïtic scripts represent two of the worst-case scenarios with regard to decipherment.
    - The two are about evenly matched in terms of the five pillars. Each has an ample and varied corpus; the type of script is clear in both cases; we know a great deal about their cultural

contexts; and both writing systems have biscripts. The starting conditions with respect to these four pillars are about as good as we could hope for.

○ Only the language pillar is wanting. The Etruscan and Meroïtic languages are both isolates, meaning that they have no known relatives or descendants, and they are both poorly recorded, meaning that there are no surviving dictionaries or grammars to help us interpret them. Language is the only thing holding up their decipherment—but that's no small thing!

Etruscan Civilization

- The Etruscan civilization of northwest Italy arose in about 800 B.C., some 50 years before the traditional date of the founding of Rome in 753 B.C. The Etruscans were at their height in 500 B.C. Like many of their contemporaries in the Mediterranean, the Etruscans were seafarers and traders.

- Many trade goods and opportunities came by way of merchant ships from Greek and Phoenician civilization. And it was by virtue of these same sea routes that the Etruscans first came into contact with the Greek alphabet, which they borrowed and adapted to serve their language. In turn, the early Romans were heavily influenced by the Etruscans, from whom they borrowed their alphabet.

- It's easy to see—both from the shape and orientation of signs and from their sound values—that the Etruscans must have borrowed their alphabet from the Greeks rather than the Phoenicians. For one thing, the Etruscan alphabet includes the five cardinal signs for vowels, a Greek innovation, as well as such characteristic Greek signs as Φ and X.

- The earliest Greek writing ran from right to left, and later Greek was sometimes written in boustrophedon, with alternating left-to-right and right-to-left lines. Whenever the script ran from right to left, the letters would be rotated 180 degrees from what we think of as the normal orientation. This reading order left a remnant in the typical orientation of Etruscan letters, which favored the right-to-left order and orientation.

- There were also several sound changes in adapting the Greek alphabet to the Etruscan language. Note that the Greek letter *B* was borrowed by Etruscan but not as the sound /b/, which apparently didn't exist in the Etruscan language; rather, it was used for the sound /f/, for which there was no sign in Greek. These kinds of changes during script borrowing are common.

- We know where the Etruscan alphabet came from (the Greek alphabet) and where it went (the Roman alphabet). As a result, we can read almost every word of Etruscan aloud with a fair degree of certainty. Unfortunately, we understand very little of it.

- Despite its early importance, Etruria was completed dominated by Rome by 300 B.C. Within the next 300 years, the region had become fully assimilated to metropolitan Roman culture, abandoning the Etruscan language in both public and private sectors in favor of Latin.

The Etruscan Language

- There are many short bilingual tomb inscriptions in Etruscan and Latin, as well as several explanations of Etruscan words and names in Latin sources. Three gold plaques discovered at the Etruscan port of Pyrgi in 1964 also provide a lengthy

Etruscan women were frequently buried with bronze mirrors whose backs were decorated with elaborate mythological scenes.

bilingual temple dedication in Phoenician and Etruscan, dating to about 500 B.C. But that's all we have, and there are no dictionaries or grammars.

- Some picture biscripts are available, but they don't add anything to our knowledge of the Etruscan language. They do, however, attest to the strong cultural influence of Greek mythology. Bronze mirrors buried with Etruscan women also show mythological scenes.

- The Etruscan language and writing system were eventually abandoned in favor of Latin and the Roman alphabet, and Etruscan culture was similarly absorbed by Roman imperial culture. But the Etruscans have left behind a rich legacy. The classical myths we know today have passed down to us via the Romans with a decidedly Etruscan flavor.

Meroïtic Civilization

- The Kushite or Meroïtic civilization was one of the most important early states of Sub-Saharan Africa. Its origins go back to the 3rd millennium B.C., but it entered written history (through references in Egyptian hieroglyphs) only in the 8th century B.C. In the late 8th century, Kushite kings conquered Egypt itself, founding its 25th dynasty.

- The Nubian kings portrayed themselves as devout worshipers of Amun and restorers of the glory of Egypt after a series of disastrous civil wars. They ruled Egypt for almost 100 years but were pushed back by the Assyrians in the 7th century B.C. Returning to Kush, they built great pyramid fields modeled after those at Giza.

- In their home country, the Kushites began recording their history in Egyptian hieroglyphs, erecting *stelae* similar to those in Egypt and burying inscribed objects in their tombs. By about 300 B.C., however, they had innovated a writing system of their own: an *abugida* (a mixed script with alphabetic and syllabic characters).

- The Kushites abandoned Egyptian hieroglyphs in favor of their new script, which they used to write their own language. They continued to do so for almost 750 years, until the mid-4th century A.D. More than 1,000 Meroïtic texts are known. Most of them are on stone, but there are also texts on ceramic sherds, papyrus, and wood. Formulaic funerary inscriptions constitute more than half of the known corpus, although there are also some lengthy royal texts on stelae.

- The Meroïtic script was abandoned only in the 4th century, as Kush disintegrated into three smaller kingdoms and converted to Christianity. It's unclear precisely why Meroïtic was abandoned, but it may have had more to do with the slow demise of the Meroïtic language under pressure from Coptic Christian culture than with script death itself.

The Meroïtic Script

- In the mid-19th century, the Egyptologist Karl Richard Lepsius recognized that Meroïtic had only 23 signs (not including a common word divider) and that it had both a hieroglyphic and a cursive variant. On that basis, Lepsius argued that the script was most likely an alphabet, and until recently, most scholars concurred. But recent work suggests that it was a partial syllabary, technically known as an abugida.

- The Meroïtic sound values used by most scholars today derive largely from the decipherment presented by Francis Llewellyn Griffith early in the 20th century. Griffith began by comparing hieroglyphic and cursive inscriptions to discover equivalencies. Close study allowed Griffith to equate all 23 hieroglyphic signs with their cursive equivalents.

- Griffith next turned to an important biscript, published earlier by Lepsius and recorded on the base of a sacred wooden boat. The texts contained two sets of royal names encircled in cartouches—one set in Egyptian hieroglyphs, the other in Meroïtic hieroglyphs. The Egyptian cartouches had been known since the late 19th century to provide the names of the Kushitic king Netekamani and his queen, Amanitare.

- ○ By comparing the Meroïtic inscriptions, Griffith was able to propose the consonantal values M, N, T, K and R, as well as the vowel signs I and E. The similarity of some of these signs to their sources in the Egyptian script was immediately striking.

- ○ But other Meroïtic signs were quite different. Some resembled Egyptian signs whose values they didn't share, and some seemed to be new creations.

- ○ These discoveries remind us that it's only after a successful decipherment on the basis of biscripts, bilinguals, or other constraints that we can appreciate which signs were borrowed and which were not. Formal comparisons never constitute independent evidence for decipherment.

- • Griffith went on to test and refine his sign values in other contexts, but because the underlying language remains unknown, scholars have largely had to satisfy themselves with reading the personal names of rulers in Meroïtic hieroglyphs, counting themselves lucky whenever those same names also appeared in Egyptian hieroglyphic inscriptions in Meroë.

- • From time to time, a Greek connection of some kind has definitely been entertained, particularly by scholars uncomfortable with the idea of the independent invention of vowels by the Greeks and the Kushites. Certainly, the idea that the vowels of the Meroïtic abugida might owe something to the Greek alphabet cannot be entirely ruled out, but there is no positive evidence for it either, not in the form of the Meroïtic vowel signs or in the specifics of their syllabic usage.

- • Today, scholars know only the rough meanings of about 26 words in Meroïtic, all of them derived from Egyptian/Meroïtic biscripts and contextual analysis of the inscriptions. They include such words as *malo* ("good"), *at* ("bread"), *ato* ("water"), *mak* ("god"), and *kandake* ("queen"). Unfortunately, these words don't resemble any known language of the region, either modern or ancient.

- As with Etruscan, a picture of the Meroïtic speakers nonetheless emerges even from this poorly understood script. They were more Egyptian than the Egyptians and eventually developed their own writing system to record their histories, only abandoning it after waves of foreign invasion and the new social, political, and economic realities of Christianization.

Important Terms

abugida (or **alphasyllabary**): A writing system composed of a mixture of consonantal signs and syllabic signs, such as Meroïtic and Devanagari. The term was coined by Peter Daniels (1990).

stela (pl. **stelae**): A common format for carved monuments, the stela is a freestanding, dressed stone slab erected in a public space to commemorate important events.

Suggested Reading

Bonfante and Bonfante, *The Etruscan Language*.

Bonfante, *Etruscan*.

Griffith, "Meroitic Inscriptions."

Melikian, "The Mysteries of Meroe."

Pallottino, *The Etruscans*.

Possehl, *Indus Age*.

Rilly, "The Linguistic Position of Meroitic."

Rilly and de Voogt, *The Meroitic Language and Writing System*.

Robinson, *Lost Languages*.

Rowan, "Meroitic—An Afroasiatic Language?"

Shinnie, *Meroe.*

Welsby, *The Kingdom of Kush.*

Questions to Consider

1. What will you say the next time someone tells you about a new computer program or novel analytical that is about to "crack" one of the undeciphered scripts mentioned in this lecture? What would have to change for Etruscan or Meroïtic to be deciphered? What about the Indus script discussed in Lecture 9?

2. Did you know that the English words *person* and *people* can both be traced back to Etruscan as early borrowings by Latin? What else do we owe to this remarkable people? Should we be concerned that their language has vanished so utterly? Why or why not?

3. What do you think about the preoccupation of the Kushite pharaohs of Egypt with portraying themselves as "more Egyptian than the Egyptians"? Is this radically different from the concerns of politicians today, roughly 2,700 years later? Why or why not?

Han'gŭl, Tengwar, and Other Featural Scripts
Lecture 22

M any scripts around the world have been consciously designed, usually by a single individual or a small group of people, over a short period of time, and with specific aims and intentions. What's fascinating is that most of them contain unmistakable internal evidence of their artificial invention. The linguist Geoffrey Sampson coined the term *featural script* for these writing systems. Featural scripts are highly phonetic scripts—alphabets, abugidas, or syllabaries—in which sign shapes are not arbitrarily related to sound (as they are in what we might call "natural" writing systems) but, instead, encode the phonetic features of the sounds they represent. In this lecture, we'll look at several featural scripts, including Korean Han'gŭl, shorthand, and fictional alphabets.

Characteristics of Featural Scripts

- *Featural scripts* include some national writing systems in daily use, such as Korean *Han'gŭl* and the Canadian Inuktitut syllabary; idealistic alphabets, such as Lodwick's universal alphabet; several kinds of *shorthand*; and fictional alphabets designed for fantasy and science fiction, of which J.R.R. Tolkien's are perhaps the most well-known.

- Despite their superficial differences and their different uses, all these writing systems betray their intentional design in everything from structural organization to paradigmatic relationships between sign form and pronunciation. These are precisely the features that natural scripts do not show, clearly indicating that most writing systems were not purposefully designed in this way.

- Both structural and morphological evidence sets featural scripts apart. Structurally, the arrangement of signs in featural scripts and the relationships between them aren't arbitrary, as they are in most writing systems, but deeply purposeful. With regard to morphology, the outward form or appearance of signs isn't pictorial, abstract, or arbitrary, as it is in many of the scripts we've seen so far, but deeply patterned, with formal connections between signs representing similar sounds.

- Many featural scripts are structurally organized into grids or charts based on articulatory phonetics, that is, the way sounds are made by the human mouth. For example, in a featural script, the signs for *b* (a voiced bilabial plosive) and *p* (a voiceless bilabial plosive) will be grouped together, and *p* will also be grouped with other voiceless plosives, such as *t* and *k*. This phonetic organization is anything but arbitrary.

- Featural scripts aren't just structurally organized into groups of signs representing similar kinds of sounds; the signs themselves are designed to reveal these groupings. Formal features, such as sign shape, orientation, and the addition of diacritical marks, all reveal phonetic connections between signs.

Lodwick's Universal Alphabet

- Francis Lodwick (1619–1694) was a Dutch merchant living in London and an avid pioneer of spelling reform. Like many immigrants, he was disenchanted by the mismatch between English spelling and pronunciation. He first proposed several spelling reforms, but he soon learned that the inertia of writing has both traditional and practical dimensions that make reform difficult.

- Recognizing that simply repurposing the Latin alphabet made it hard to avoid the impression that his new spellings weren't just errors, Lodwick decided to create a universal script. In his 1686 paper introducing his new alphabet, Lodwick outlined his three aims: (1) to facilitate learning for children, (2) to facilitate the recording of other languages, and (3) to serve as a standard reference for the sounds of a language.

- Lodwick expressed one rule for his new writing system: "that no Character have more than one Sound, nor any one Sound be expressed by more than one Character." This meant that such sounds as /f/ wouldn't be represented with the letters *f*, *ph*, or *-gh* (as they are in English) but with only a single sign.

- Lodwick's universal alphabet separated consonants and vowels. The consonants were the same size as Roman consonants, but the vowels were smaller, designed to appear above consonants, similar to accent marks. Lodwick also grouped sounds in columns, putting together the bilabial consonants (*b*, *p*, *m*), **alveolar** consonants (*d*, *t*, *n*), and so on.

J.R.R. Tolkien's Writing Systems

- J.R.R. Tolkien was a professional linguist and a specialist in the history of Germanic languages and literature, both alphabetic and runic. In *The Hobbit*, first published in 1937, Tolkien used Anglo-Saxon runes as a kind of code for Modern English. Tolkien also invented several writing systems of his own, including the cursive script known as **Tengwar** or Tîw (meaning "letters") and the angular characters designed for cutting into wood, stone, or metal known as **Certar** or Cirth (meaning "runes").

- Tolkien used the Tengwar script on his original cover for *The Lord of the Rings*, recording the ominous opening lines of the ring poem: "*Ash nazg durbatulûk*" ("One ring to rule them all"). He even gave his fictional scripts a fictional inventor, Rúmil.

- Both Tengwar and Certar are featural scripts. Characters representing sounds of similar **place of articulation** or **manner of articulation** have formal properties that reflect this. Tolkien provides charts and full descriptions of his writing systems in appendix E of *The Lord of the Rings*. In these charts, he makes it clear that his scripts aren't organized only by place and manner of articulation but that the signs themselves formally signal their phonetic relationships to one another.

Korean Han'gŭl

- As you might remember from Lecture 5, the Koreans initially adopted the Chinese script, which they used to write Korean for more than 1,000 years. But in 1443, King Sejong (r. 1419–1450) produced a new featural alphabet that would eventually be called Han'gŭl, Korean for "great script."

- The Han'gŭl alphabet has 24 signs: 14 consonants and 10 vowels. Han'gŭl signs don't appear in simple linear sequence, as ours do; instead, they're grouped into blocks representing whole syllables. This is a formal influence of Chinese characters. Until the 1980s, Korean was usually written from right to left in vertical columns, just as Chinese once was. Today, however, the majority of texts are written from left to right in horizontal lines.

- King Sejong was motivated to create Han'gŭl because Chinese characters were a complex and cumbersome way to write the Korean language, which is very different from Mandarin Chinese. The characters took a long time to master and were, therefore, always the domain of aristocrats, whereas Han'gŭl was designed for everyone.

- By the 19th century, Han'gŭl had been adopted as an official script. Today, Korean is still written in a mixed script that uses Chinese characters for borrowed Chinese vocabulary and Han'gŭl for native words. North Koreans write exclusively in Han'gŭl, and South Koreans are moving in the same direction.

Shorthand and Featural Scripts of Canada
- Phonetic scripts developed for stenography in the 19th century included Pitman, Gregg, and Sweet shorthand—all of which were featural scripts. In 1840, James Evans, a missionary working in northeastern Canada, was inspired by Pitman shorthand to create a syllabary for the Ojibwe language.
  - The core of the syllabary is nine consonantal symbols that could be rotated in four directions to signal different associated vowels. A diacritic (a superscript dot) could also be used to mark vowels as long.

o The script was featural in that all syllables with the same consonant shared the same basic shape, while all syllables with the same vowel shared the same orientation. But nothing unites consonants that are similar with respect to place or manner of articulation; thus, it's not quite as featural as the other scripts we've seen.

- Evans later adapted his script to write Cree, and others adapted it for the Inuktitut language. This became one of the official scripts of the Inuit Cultural Institute of Canada in 1976, and it's still used on a daily basis in the Canadian territory of Nunavut.

Darius the Great and Old Persian

- In Lecture 15, we studied the Behistun trilingual. Among its more remarkable boasts is Darius the Great's claim that he designed the Achaemenid syllabary. Because the Achaemenid script first appeared during Darius's reign, some scholars have believed this claim, but more recent scholarship is skeptical.

- The script seems mature, with none of the hesitations, inconsistencies, or errors one might expect of a new system. It may have existed for some time on perishable media, with the Behistun monument serving as its public debut. Still, scholars have wondered whether Darius commissioned his scribes to produce a nationalistic Achaemenid script, with the king taking credit.

- Despite the debate, no one has considered the Old Persian syllabary from the perspective of featural scripts. If Darius's claim is true, then the Old Persian syllabary was invented by a single individual (or a small group), over a short period of time, and with a single purpose in mind. If it could be shown that the Old Persian syllabary also had hallmarks of other featural scripts, Darius's claim might be at least partially validated.
  o We don't know about the organizational principles of the Old Persian syllabary, because we don't have a list of signs showing their order or arrangement, if any. But a close look at the signs themselves reveals no pattern linking the form of the signs to

their sound values. Sign form seems to be completely arbitrary, and the script as a whole seems indistinguishable from other natural scripts.

○ These facts seem to cast doubt on Darius's claim. But then again, perhaps Old Persian was like the Cherokee syllabary invented by Chief Sequoyah in the early 19th century or the Bamum syllabary of Cameroon invented by King Njoya in 1896, both of which were designed to seem natural.

Conclusions about Featural Scripts

- As we've seen, the objectives of those who developed phonetic scripts are broad. For spelling reformers, such as Lodwick, idealistic concerns predominated. For Tolkien, a secret code in which to keep his journals and in which his linguist's mind could have free rein eventually gave way to world building in fiction. For King Sejong, there seems to have been a complex mix of idealistic, practical, and nationalistic concerns at work.

- What shines through in all these examples is the versatility of writing generally. And like ancient scripts, invented ones don't seem to have been motivated only by their first documented uses. Rather, it's their structural features that prove most enlightening. Featural scripts were designed to be featural scripts. Beyond that, a featural script can be applied to write any language, just as any other script can.

- Whatever the motives for their invention, the many featural scripts that have been used to record English serve as a useful reminder that language is not the same thing as writing. When we also remember that Old English was written in runes and that Modern English can be written in Braille, we're less likely to equate our language with our writing system and perhaps more willing to entertain options for its improvement or alteration in the future.

alveolar: Refers to a sound made by touching the tip of the tongue to the alveolar ridge behind the upper teeth (e.g., *t*, *d*, and *n*).

Certar (also **Cirth**): J.R.R. Tolkien's runic-inspired featural script.

featural script: A highly phonetic script in which sign organization and sign form are not arbitrary but, instead, encode phonetic features, such as place and manner of articulation, as in Korean Han'gŭl and Tolkien's Tengwar and Certar. The term was coined by Geoffrey Sampson (1985).

Han'gŭl (also **Hangul**): The 15th-century featural alphabet developed for Korean by King Sejong.

manner of articulation: Refers to the way in which air pressure, vocal cords, and other features help to produce a sound (e.g., plosive, fricative, nasal).

place (or **point**) **of articulation**: Refers to the location in the mouth where a sound is made or the parts of the mouth responsible for a sound (e.g., bilabial, dental, alveolar, palatal, velar, glottal).

shorthand: A method of rapid writing by means of abbreviation and phonetic signs, especially for taking dictation. The most popular systems were designed by Isaac Pitman and John R. Gregg in the late 19th century; both are featural scripts.

Tengwar (also **Tîw**): A calligraphic featural script invented by J.R.R. Tolkien.

Suggested Reading

Abercrombie, *Studies in Phonetics and Linguistics* (especially pp. 46–54 for Lodwick's universal alphabet of 1686.)

Campbell, *Historical Linguistics*.

Kuhrt, *The Persian Empire*.

Lodwick, "An Essay Towards an Universal Alphabet."

MacMahon, "Henry Sweet's System of Shorthand."

Sampson, *Writing Systems*.

Smith, "The Alphabet of Rúmil."

———, "Pre-Fëanorian Alphabets, Part I."

———, "The Quenya Alphabet."

Tolkien, *The Silmarillion*.

———, *The Lord of the Rings*.

Walker and Sarbaugh, "The Early History of the Cherokee Syllabary."

Questions to Consider

1. What is a featural script? In what sense are these kinds of scripts clearly artificial, showing the hand of a single inventor (or a small group)?

2. If you have a copy of *The Lord of the Rings*, compare the Certar table from appendix E to the fuþark discussed in Lecture 4. Do any signs have the same shapes and values in the two systems? How do the featural qualities of the Certar conspire to make this a haphazard relationship at best?

3. Did Darius the Great invent Old Persian cuneiform? Consider the classical arguments both in favor of and against the king's claim. Does the perspective afforded by featural scripts shift the balance in favor of one or the other position? Why or why not? What kind of evidence would be needed to decisively test Darius's claim?

Medium and Message
Lecture 23

The Canadian philosopher Marshall McLuhan is known for his counterintuitive axiom "The medium is the message." McLuhan's idea was that a medium (or a context) affects society and civilization not only by the message (or content) it delivers but through its own characteristics and relationships. McLuhan argued that medium was an important focus of study in its own right and that a careful examination of media might allow us to detect the unanticipated consequences of new technologies we might miss by privileging content alone. Early civilizations definitely saw McLuhan's interrelated and interdependent connection of medium and message as revealed in the terms we use for writing implements, the act of writing, and the media on which writing appears.

Writing Implements, Writing, and Media

- The word *pen* comes from Old French *penne*, meaning a "quill pen." In turn, the French word came from Classical Latin *penna*, which meant "feather." The word *pencil* comes from Old French *pincel*, meaning "paintbrush." *Pen* and *pencil* refer to different kinds of writing implements today, but their etymologies reflect the influx of continental scribal culture into England in the wake of the Norman Conquest, when writing was done with quills or brushes dipped in ink.

- In Lecture 4, we saw that the English word *writing* comes from Old English *wrítan*, meaning "to cut, inscribe." Interestingly, the word *book* comes from Old English *bōc*, which primarily meant "beech tree." Evidently, the first Germanic runes were cut into wood, or *wrítan on bōc*. Later, *wrítan* was extended from carving to inking, and *bōc*, from "beech," to "writing tablet," to "book."
  - Similarly, the word ***codex*** comes from Late Latin *cōdex* (Classical Latin *caudex*), which meant "tree trunk." Today, a codex refers to a manuscript made of a number of bound sheets of paper, parchment, or vellum. Usually, codices are stacked

and bound at one edge, like a book, but sometimes they're continuous and folded accordion-style. Codex technology was developed by the Romans from wooden writing tablets.

○ At first, these tablets were singular objects, but they began to be laced together with sinew. By the 1st century A.D., this began to be done with parchment, vellum, or papyrus. With the change in technology, the word *caudex* changed its meaning from "tree trunk," to "block of wood," to "writing tablet," and eventually, to a specific kind of manuscript book made of lighter sheets of treated animal hide, papyrus paper, or pulp paper.

• Like so many of our other terms for the written culture that entered England with the Norman Conquest, the word *paper* can be traced through French back to Classical Latin *papyrus*. The Latin word already referred to paper in the conventional sense, but Latin had itself borrowed the term from Greek (*papyros*), where it specifically referred to the papyrus plant and only secondarily to the writing material made from it.

○ The Greek word *papyros* clearly didn't originate in Greek. In fact, Greek had two words for papyrus and its products, the other being *byblos*. Both of these seem to be early loanwords from Semitic, with the latter a clear reference to the Phoenician city of Byblos.

○ This indicates that papyrus paper must have been disseminated into the Mediterranean by Phoenician traders, from whom the Greeks picked up both the product and the word.

○ Comparative linguistics shows us that *papyros* and *byblos* are actually the same word. Perhaps Greek borrowed this word at two different times, from two Phoenician dialects, or from two distinct Semitic languages.

○ However the word *byblos* came into Greek, its meaning eventually expanded to signify "scroll" and "manuscript." When the book was introduced to the Greek-speaking world, the diminutive *biblion* (literally "small scroll") was coined to refer to this new item. From *biblion* come the English words *bibliophile*, *bibliography*, and *bibliomania*.

○ The plural of Greek *biblion* is *biblia*. Latin borrowed this Greek word to refer to the Greek books (plural) of the New Testament, from which we get our word *Bible*. Thus, the word *Bible* traces its origin to the word *papyrus*, which was itself one of the names of an ancient Phoenician city!

Manufacturing Papyrus Paper
- Papyrus is a tall, aquatic sedge native to central Africa and the Nile valley. It once grew abundantly in Egypt and was eaten and used to make rope and reed boats. The process of manufacturing paper from papyrus is long and elaborate and must have originally involved a great deal of trial and error.

- After the mature papyrus plants were harvested, the core of the stalk was sliced into long, thin strips. After soaking in water, the papyrus strips were laid out in slightly overlapping fashion until the

© Getty Images/Photos.com/Thinkstock.

For more than 4,000 years, papyrus scrolls dominated the publishing industry; the demise of the scroll carries a lesson for us now, in the age of the e-book.

desired sheet length was reached. Then, a second set of strips was laid over the first at right angles. The double-layered paper was then placed between linen and either pounded or pressed to remove the water. Under pressure, the papyrus sap seeped out to bind the strips into a single sheet.

- After pressing, drying, and trimming, the papyrus sheets were destined for either scrolls or books. For thousands of years, individual sheets were stuck together to make long writing surfaces, which could then be rolled up into scrolls. In later times, individual papyrus sheets were simply stitched together to form a book. The earliest known paper made out of papyrus is at least 5,100 years old, dating to a time not much later than the earliest writing in Egypt.

- The Phoenicians began the international dissemination of Egyptian papyrus, but the Greeks were importing it by at least the 6th century B.C. After their founding of the Macedonian Ptolemaic dynasty in 304 B.C., the Greeks themselves were in control of paper, which they exported to the whole of the Mediterranean. This trade continued until the 12th century A.D.

The Origins of Paper
- The traditional story of the origin of paper credits Cai Lun, a eunuch at the imperial court of China in the early 2nd century A.D., who was supposed to have made the first paper from tree bark, hemp, cloth rags, and old fishing nets. However, archaeologists have discovered earlier evidence of paper at a few 2nd-century-B.C. sites in western China.

- Paper is derived from cotton, flax, wood, and other plant materials. These are soaked and sometimes heated, then shredded, macerated, and pounded into pulp before being collected on a finely woven screen and dried into sheets. The procedure is now automated, but paper has been made this way for more than 2,000 years.

- Chinese paper-making was quickly borrowed by Korea, Vietnam, and Japan, but it wasn't until the 8th and 9th centuries A.D. that it finally made its way along the Silk Road to the Muslim world, eventually arriving in Moorish Spain in the 11th century. At that time, the paper mills of Granada first introduced Europe to this new and relatively inexpensive technology, signaling the end for imported papyrus.

Other Media for Writing

- There are other media for writing, equally important in their impact on the shape and content of early writing. As mentioned in Lecture 5, it's probably the case that the first Chinese writing was painted onto small bamboo slips that were threaded together to form an early kind of codex. Although the earliest surviving examples of these bamboo codices date to the 5th century B.C., there are several clues that this practice extended at least as early as the Shang period, or about 1400 B.C.

- Increasing angularization, stylization, and simplification of early pictorial graphs is often the result of a change of medium.
  - As we noted in Lecture 3, the abundant papyrus of the Nile delta probably explains the pictorial origins of our own alphabet. As the preferred medium shifted to carving and, perhaps, also to wax tablets or clay, the pictorial script responded by becoming more rectilinear and simplified. The change of medium also led to changes in sign orientation and to experimentation with different directions of reading.

  - In a parallel fashion, early rune-carvers apparently cut runes into wood from the very beginning. This handily explains the pronounced angular forms of their Roman-derived letters and probably also motivates the rotation of some signs to make them more amenable to the new medium.

  - In Lecture 16, we saw that the highly pictorial glyphs of ancient Sumerian writing also apparently gave way to angular cuneiform as the medium changed from some perishable substrate to coarser and less responsive clay. Here, too, scholars suspect that the 90-degree rotation of early cuneiform signs was related to this shift of medium.

- Whether on papyrus, bamboo, clay, stone, or wood, there's clearly an important relationship between medium and message. It's partially deterministic, of course; how could a medium not transform what passes through it? But it isn't entirely so, and it isn't one-way only, because the need to convey writing also led to developments and alterations in the technology of writing itself.

The Technology of Writing

- Transformations in technologies of writing can usually be linked to social transformations, such as the emergence of printing at an early date in China, but its practical application only much later, in the West, where an alphabet of only 26 signs made printing practical at the same time that the growing prestige of vernacular languages created an audience. But perhaps the most visible example of this phenomenon was the demise of the papyrus scroll and the birth of the book in the context of the emergence of Christianity.

- The gradual replacement of scrolls by codices has been called "the most significant development in the history of the book before the invention of printing." Several scholars have noted that the spread of the codex can be closely linked to the rise of Christianity, which adopted this format for the Greek texts of the New Testament.

- One theory to explain the early Christian enthusiasm for the codex is that Christians repudiated the pagan contents of Egyptian papyrus scrolls, embracing the new codex technology as a departure from the past. It seems more likely, however, that the practical and economic advantages of codex technology won the day.

- At its demise at the close of the 1st millennium A.D., the papyrus scroll was a venerable technology. The purely practical reasons for its passing carry an object lesson for us today, in the age of the e-book, which will, without question, eventually lead to the death of the printed book.

Important Term

codex (pl. **codices**): A bound manuscript (i.e., written by hand). Codices can be stacked and bound at one edge, like a modern book, or they can be continuous and screenfold.

Suggested Reading

Bagley, "Anyang Writing and the Origin of the Chinese Writing System."

Diringer, *The Hand-Produced Book.*

Federman, "What Is the Meaning of 'The Medium Is the Message'?"

McLuhan, *The Gutenberg Galaxy.*

———, *Understanding Media.*

Metzger, "When Did Scribes Begin to Use Writing Desks?"

Roberts and Skeat, *The Birth of the Codex.*

Robinson, *Writing and Script.*

Ryan, "Papyrus."

Yamauchi, "Review of *The Birth of the Codex.*"

Questions to Consider

1. In what ways is writing dependent on and influenced by the implements and media used to record and convey it? Is this an inevitable relationship? Why or why not?

2. What lessons does the demise of the papyrus scroll after more than 4,000 years of use hold for the future of writing?

The Future of Writing
Lecture 24

As we've seen, grammatology (or comparative writing) is a historical science. In place of controlled experiments, such sciences rely on comparison, seeking out patterns and associations in a universe of diverse phenomena to infer general laws and testing those laws on new evidence when it becomes available. This methodology allows the historical sciences to retrodict the past with remarkable accuracy. But the turbulence inherent in complex, multifaceted, and interdependent systems, such as the weather or language, greatly limits our powers of prediction. We can't predict the many possible futures of the world's writing systems, but we can make reasonable speculations about what the future might bring, founded on the careful comparisons we've made in these lectures.

From Tablets to Papyrus

- In ancient Mesopotamia, clay tablets were the *sine qua non* of writing for almost 3,200 years, that is, from about 3100 B.C. until the last cuneiform inscription was written in the late 1ˢᵗ century A.D. The technology was simple but effective.

  o Clay tablets were intentionally flat on one side and convex on the other. The flat side was inscribed first, so that when the tablet was turned over, it could lay flat, protecting the inscription. Clay tablets were usually stored on shelves to dry, where they could be easily accessed. They could be altered at will, and if they were no longer wanted, they could be recycled. If a permanent record was desired, the clay could be baked in a fire. Scribes also supplemented clay tablets with hinged tablets that had a wax-coated writing surface.

  o Without doubt, both of these media were intractable. As we've seen, they drove changes in the form of signs, their orientations, and even the direction of writing. For these reasons, scribes must have been relieved when the Neo-Assyrian emperor Tiglath-Pīlēser III adopted the Aramaic language and script in the middle of the 8th century B.C. The Aramaic script was an abjad, adapted from the Phoenician abjad, which means it had the same origin as our alphabet.

- As the years wore on, the advantages of writing an abjad on papyrus became increasingly obvious to scribes and rulers. The new script and technology finally succeeded in doing what thousands of years of conquest, reconquest, borrowing, adaptation, and imitation had never managed to do. After 3,200 years, scribes ceased writing cuneiform, adopting and adapting the Aramaic script to serve the needs of different languages and giving rise to the modern Hebrew and Arabic alphabets, among many others.

- Interestingly, the Aramaic abjad and its papyrus scrolls coexisted with the Assyrian logosyllabary and its clay tablets for almost 800 years. But again, the outcome for tablets was inevitable and for the same practical reasons that e-books will eventually phase out printed books.

- In the last lecture, we discussed the chronology and rationale for the phasing out of papyrus scrolls by codices, but this, too, was a process that took some time to complete. From the first signs of the growing popularity of codices, in the 2nd century A.D., it took about 800 years for scrolls to vanish entirely.

Printing and the Demise of the Codex

- The earliest printing was with fixed type, which means that a block of text was carved in the negative, usually on wood, and then covered with ink to create prints. This kind of printing first appeared in Han dynasty China around the beginning of the 3rd century A.D., but it wasn't adapted to paper until sometime later. Because of the desire for more Chinese texts than calligraphers could supply, woodcut printing took off particularly rapidly in Korea, Japan, and Vietnam.

- The most significant development in printing was the invention of movable type: numerous copies of the same carved or cast signs that could be redistributed to print different works.

○ Movable type was also first invented in China, in the early 11th century A.D., using porcelain, wood, and copper. The Koreans introduced bronze type in the early 13th century, but it never caught on because of the thousands of characters of Chinese writing, which made it expensive and inefficient. Instead, woodcut printing remained the most common method of Chinese printing until the modern era.

○ In the mid-15th century, Johannes Gutenberg developed the first modern movable type in Europe. He was the first to die-cast his type from pliable but durable lead, as it's still done today. The much smaller number of signs in the alphabet made metal typefaces much more practical than they were for Chinese characters.

- When the Gutenberg Bible was published in 1455, Europeans were impressed by its relatively low price (compared with manuscripts), its high quality, and its consistency. Printing swept across Europe, signaling the end of the scriptorium and the codex. But once again, there was a sizable lag between the first invention of printing and the eventual demise of codices.

- The advent of printing had other effects, too, both on the shape of our script and on its spelling conventions. Some characters that were problematic to typeset were basically discontinued. Printing also encouraged the idea of "correct" orthography—a single way that words ought to be spelled. As we've seen many times in these lectures, changes in media and the technology of writing can have unforeseen consequences in the shape, orientation, and orthographic rules of writing systems.

Keyboarding versus Handwriting

- If keyboards themselves aren't overtaken by other technologies, typing is likely to replace handwriting. Keep in mind that new writing technologies never replace older ones overnight but only gradually edge them out over hundreds of years. In that light, consider that many of us no longer write much by hand.

- Cursive instruction has all but ceased in public schools, and younger generations today write more text with their phones and laptops than they do by hand. This development is completely in keeping with what we've seen in our historical survey of writing technology: Practical new tools and media are gradually but inevitably adopted.

- As with the adoption of printing, the invention of the keyboard has led to the inventions of new signs and the innovation of new spelling conventions. The creation of emoticons

The QWERTY arrangement continues to be used, even though its original rationale—to prevent typewriter keys from jamming—is no longer an issue.

can be traced to early computing in the 1980s, and they're a useful addition to our textual repertoire. They supplement the question mark and the exclamation mark as ways to signal emotive and prosodic features of speech that are difficult to capture in writing.

- Orthographic developments in the domain of texting tend to be denigrated or even decried by language mavens as a debasement of our writing system, if not of our language itself. But such criticisms miss the fact that our writing system has never stood still. Signs and spelling practices alike have been altered, discarded, or introduced many times in the 1,000 years since *Beowulf* was written. Yet we still have an alphabet, and it still works in basically the same way.

Writing versus Machine Transcription
- The futurist William Crossman has predicted that writing itself will be phased out by the year 2050, at which point computers will be able to intelligently respond to our voices. Anyone will be able to communicate with anyone else, without ever needing to learn how to read and write. Illiteracy will vanish as a social concern.

- The anthropologist Dan Sperber agrees with the possibility that the ongoing revolution in information and communication technology might lead to the retirement of writing as an active process. That is, automatic machine transcription of speech might well replace our need to physically write things down for ourselves, even with a keyboard.

- Speech recognition software providing speech-to-text conversion still isn't quite advanced enough for what either Crossman or Sperber envisions, but it's developing rapidly, and it's not hard to imagine a near future where a writer might draft books, articles, and lectures merely by speaking to a computer.

- It is unlikely, however, that the shape of the script produced by computers will change. Whether in hardcopy, on display screens, or in retinal readouts, English will most likely continue to be visually represented by the alphabet.
    - The alphabet has now been with us for about 4,000 years, since its first invention in and around Egypt by early Semitic speakers. Since then, it has passed through the hands of the Phoenicians, Greeks, Etruscans, Romans, Normans, and Anglo-Saxons on its way to us. And each of these groups has made its own additions, alterations, and improvements.

    - The last really noteworthy improvement was the addition of vowels by the Greeks, which took place about 3,000 years ago. For this reason alone, the alphabet seems unlikely to change very much even if machine transcription of speech becomes commonplace.

- Sperber argues that even in a future world where computers do all of our writing for us, it's safe to predict that reading is here to stay. Even if everything you might want to read had already been digitized and stored in a computer, would you want to access it only by having it read to you? Would mothers no longer read to their children but have the computer do it for them?

- o There are also practical disadvantages to reading everything by listening to a computer. Listening is much slower than reading, and there's no possibility of easy backtracking by eye to double-check information presented earlier.

- o Noise is also an issue; a speaking computer voice has to be loud enough for someone to hear, and the computer has to be able to hear its user.

- An understanding of the root causes of illiteracy shows that even the demise of writing, as in Crossman's vision, would probably do little to correct it.
  - o Literacy is determined by economic, social, and political factors. Low literacy in African countries and in Afghanistan and Pakistan is the result of crushing poverty, repressive social policies, and a lack of political unity or, at least, of political clout for would-be reformers.

  - o From this perspective, it's difficult to see how Crossman's golden age of talking computers could ever solve the problem of illiteracy, because neither the technological infrastructure nor the fiscal resources to take advantage of this kind of innovation exist in the places that have the lowest literacy rates today.

- Writing is only a little more than 5,000 years old, but in that relatively brief time, it has become integral to the way we function and relate to one another. Writing has changed, to be certain, and its changes and developments are directly linked to the story of civilization around the globe. Thus, it seems safe to predict that wherever human civilization goes, writing will always be with us.

Suggested Reading

Chiera, *They Wrote on Clay*.

Common Core State Standards Initiative, *Common Core State Standards for English Language Arts and Literacy*.

Crossman, *VIVO [Voice-In/Voice-Out]: The Coming Age of Talking Computers*.

Crystal, *Txtng: The Gr8 Db8*.

Gelb, *A Study of Writing*.

Geller, "The Last Wedge."

Malik, *Summary Human Development Report, 2013*.

Robinson, *Writing and Script*.

Sperber, "The Future of Writing."

Webb-Pressler, "The Handwriting Is on the Wall."

Questions to Consider

1. Now that you've completed this course, how have your perspectives on writing changed?

2. What do you think are the most significant interconnections among writing systems, the technology of writing (writing implements and media), and civilization?

3. What do you think will be the future of writing? Are you convinced that digital media will eventually supplant printed books? Why or why not?

Glossary

abbreviation: A conventional incomplete spelling of a word (e.g., English *Mr.* for *Mister*). Abbreviations can seem like errors, but they're usually systematic and codified. For instance, the Linear B, Mayan, and Aztec scripts routinely omit the spelling out of final consonants.

abjad (or **consonantary**): A writing system composed of consonantal signs only, such as Proto-Sinaitic and Phoenician. The term was coined by Peter Daniels (1990).

abugida (or **alphasyllabary**): A writing system composed of a mixture of consonantal signs and syllabic signs, such as Meroïtic and Devanagari. The term was coined by Peter Daniels (1990).

acrophony: Process whereby a phonetic sign originates from the initial sounds of a logogram.

agentive noun: Denotes a person, animal, or thing that performs a specified action or activity (e.g., *worker, baker*). In English, agentive nouns can be derived from verbs by adding *-er*. In Mayan, this is done by adding *aj-* (e.g., *ajtz'ihb*, "writer, scribe").

'aleph: The first letter of the Hebrew alphabet, representing a glottal plosive consonant ([ʔ]). The Hebrew sign derives from Proto-Sinaitic, where it depicts an ox (Semitic: * *'ālp*).

allograph: Refers to the relationship between two or more graphically distinct signs that carry identical reading values. From a synchronic perspective, allographs are signs that are freely interchangeable. From a diachronic perspective, such signs are often the result of either sound change (where signs of different origin come to convey the same sound) or graphic divergence (where a sign takes on two different forms over time).

alphabet: A writing system composed of a mixture of consonantal and vocalic signs.

altar: An offering table used in ceremonies.

alveolar: Refers to a sound made by touching the tip of the tongue to the alveolar ridge behind the upper teeth (e.g., *t*, *d*, and *n*).

aspiration: Refers to a plosive sound made with forceful exhalation of breath, such as Greek *p^h*. Because Latin did not have this sound, it borrowed Greek *p^h* as *f*, accounting for the English pronunciation of such Greek-derived words as *physics* (Greek: *p^{h}usikē*) and *Philip* (Greek: *p^{h}illipos*).

bilabial: Refers to a sound made by pressing both lips together (e.g., *p*, *b*, and *m*).

bilingual: An inscription containing two (or more) distinct languages, whether written in the same or different scripts. In cases where more than two languages are involved, scholars occasionally refer to the inscriptions as trilingual, quadrilingual, multilingual, and so on.

biscript: An inscription containing two (or more) distinct scripts, whether recording the same or different languages. In cases where more than two scripts are involved, scholars occasionally refer to them as triscripts, quadriscripts, multiscripts, and so on.

boustrophedon: Literally "ox turning (as it plows)," from Greek *bous* ("ox") and *strophē-* ("turn"); refers to the alternating right-to-left and left-to-right reading order (and sign reversals) of sequent lines in such scripts as the early Greek alphabet.

caption: A short text adjacent to an illustrated figure or object, which it names or describes.

cartouche: An oval encircling a group of Egyptian hieroglyphs and providing one of the names of the pharaoh.

case ending: An inflectional ending on a noun, adjective, or pronoun that expresses the semantic relationship of the word to other words in the sentence. Typical cases include accusative (direct object), dative (indirect object), and genitive (possession or close association).

Certar (also **Cirth**): J.R.R. Tolkien's runic-inspired featural script.

character: A complex sign in Chinese writing, most often composed of a phonetic sign and a semantic sign, but other combinations are also known.

code: A secret message. Codes are broken by code breakers (also cryptanalysts or cryptographers). Despite some overlap in methodology, code breaking is not decipherment.

codex (pl. **codices**): A bound manuscript (i.e., written by hand). Codices can be stacked and bound at one edge, like a modern book, or they can be continuous and screenfold.

cognate: The similarity of words in two different languages due to chance, to one language borrowing a word from the other, or to shared descent from a common ancestor, in which case the words are said to be cognate.

comparative method: The method by which historical linguists compare related words in several related languages (i.e., cognates) in order to deduce the form and meaning of a word in their shared common ancestor.

complex sign (or **compound sign**, **sign compound**): A graphic unit with its own reading value, visually consisting of two or more otherwise independent signs. A relational unit is a special kind of complex sign.

consonant: A speech sound in which the breath is at least partly obstructed and which cannot form the nucleus of a syllable on its own (e.g., *p*).

consonantal sign: A phonetic sign representing a consonant, as in an abjad.

constraint: Refers to a useful clue in decipherment, such as a picture biscript or two historically related scripts sharing signs of the same form and value.

Cretan hieroglyphic: An undeciphered pictorial script from Crete, dating to c. 2200–1700 B.C.

cuneiform: Any of a large group of Near Eastern writing systems having wedge-shaped characters. Some of these scripts are historically related (e.g., Sumerian, Babylonian, and Hittite); others are merely visually influenced by them (e.g., Ugaritic, Old Persian).

cursive: Generally speaking, *cursive* refers to writing with joined characters, as in the longhand once taught in grade school. But some scripts designed for rapid writing with ink on paper are also known as *cursive*, such as Egyptian demotic, Japanese *hiragana*, and Aramaic abjad.

Cypriotic script (or **Cypriotic syllabary**): A syllabary from Cyprus, recording a dialect of ancient Greek and dating to c. 800–250 B.C. This script is related to both Linear A and Linear B.

Cyrillic: A Greek-derived alphabet named after the late-9th-century Greek missionary Saint Cyril and now used to write Russian, Ukrainian, and other Slavic languages.

damnatio memoriae: Latin for "condemnation of memory," referring to a punishment of traitors by the Roman Senate, whose names were stricken from historical records.

decipherment: A complete account of sign use in a writing system, including details of sign types, orthography (i.e., spelling rules), and abbreviational conventions.

demotic: A visually simplified Egyptian logophonetic script developed in the 7th century B.C. One of the three scripts on the Rosetta Stone.

dental: Refers to a sound made by touching the bottom lip to the upper teeth (e.g., *f*, *v*), or the tip of the tongue to the teeth (e.g., voiced and voiceless *th*).

determinative: See **semantic sign**.

diacritic: A sign that does not have a phonetic value of its own but signals a change in value of signs with which it is associated. In French, when the letter *c* appears with a cedilla (ç), it is no longer pronounced [k] but, rather, [s], as in the word *façade*.

dialect: A variant form of a language, usually defined by region, class, or socioeconomic group and distinguished from other variants by pronunciation, vocabulary, and grammar.

digraphia: Refers to a situation in which two different scripts are used by the same community, usually for different purposes. Modeled on the linguistic term *diglossia*, referring to the different sociopolitical functions of two languages in a single community.

diphthong: Complex vowels made up of two distinct vowels merged into a single syllable (e.g., the medial vowel *ai* in Modern English *knight*).

epigrapher (also **epigraphist**): Specialist in the study of writing systems.

epistemology: The theory of knowledge, particularly with regard to its methods, validity, and scope. The investigation of what distinguishes justified belief from opinion or tradition.

ethnonym: Proper name referring to an ethnic group.

etymology: The origin of a word and the historical development of its meaning.

featural script: A highly phonetic script in which sign organization and sign form are not arbitrary but, instead, encode phonetic features, such as place and manner of articulation, as in Korean Han'gŭl and Tolkien's Tengwar and Certar. The term was coined by Geoffrey Sampson (1985).

frequency analysis: Study of the repetition of signs or sign groups in a text in order to draw conclusions based on the known frequencies of letters and words in the language it represents.

fricative: A consonant sound made through continuous expulsion of air past the point of articulation (e.g., *f* and *sh* [š]). Contrast with **plosive**.

gender marking: System by which nouns in a language carry special endings or require distinctive pronoun, adjective, and article forms. In Indo-European languages, the genders are often masculine, feminine, and neuter. For example: German *der Löffel* ("the spoon"), *die Gabel* ("the fork"), and *das Messer* ("the knife").

Germanic: A subgroup of the Indo-European family of languages that includes German, Dutch, Frisian, Swedish, Icelandic, and English, among others.

glottal: Refers to a sound made with the glottis (the part of the larynx consisting of the vocal cords and the slitlike opening between them), such as fricative [h] and plosive [ʔ] (Hebrew *'aleph*).

glyph: A convenient term for signs in any hieroglyphic script, abbreviated from hieroglyph.

grammatology: The comparative study of writing systems. The term was coined by Ignace Gelb (1952). A student of comparative writing is a grammatologist.

grapheme: See **sign**.

Great Vowel Shift: The 15th-century sound change that caused Middle English long vowels in stressed syllables to raise or become diphthongs, transforming the pronunciation of *knight* from *niːt* to *nait*. In Old English, the word was pronounced *knixt*, where *x* represents the voiceless velar fricative.

Grimm's law: A complex series of sound changes, first described by Jacob Grimm in 1822, that turned Proto-Indo-European *p* into Germanic *f*, among other related changes. Hence, Latin *pater* (which didn't undergo the change) compared to English *father* (which did).

Han'gŭl (also **Hangul**): The 15th-century featural alphabet developed for Korean by King Sejong.

Hànzì (also **Hanzi**): Literally, "Han sign"; the Mandarin term for Chinese characters.

haplography: A common abbreviational convention whereby repeating signs are omitted in writing, as in Mayan **ka-wa** for *kakaw* ("chocolate") and **u-ne** for *unen* ("baby").

hieratic: An early Egyptian logophonetic script designed for painting on papyrus. Replaced in most secular contexts by the demotic script in the 7th century B.C.

hieroglyph: Literally "sacred carving" (from Greek); now refers to single signs in a hieroglyphic script. Initially applied only to Egyptian but now freely used to describe many pictorial logophonetic scripts, such as Hittite (Luwian), Mayan, and Aztec.

hiragana: Japanese syllabary used to write inflectional endings on verbs and adjectives (behaving as phonetic complements) and to write grammatical particles and miscellaneous words that have no *kanji* (see below) or whose *kanji* are obscure.

historiography: The comparison and contrast of historical records to resolve biases and contradictions.

ideographic script: Refers to a writing system composed entirely of ideograms, that is, signs conveying meaning rather than sound. A conceptual category only because there are no such scripts. Grammatologists no longer consider *ideogram* a useful term.

Indo-European: The large language family now occupying most of Europe, Iran, and India and including English, Latin, Greek, and Sanskrit. The common ancestor of these languages probably originated on the northern steppes of the Black Sea and is known as Proto-Indo-European.

inflectional language (or **synthetic language**): A language in which the grammatical relationships between words in a sentence are determined by inflections (such as case endings). Some languages, such as Nahuatl, are what might be called hyperinflectional, building lengthy words out of the agglutination of many distinct morphemes.

International Phonetic Alphabet (or **IPA**): An internationally recognized set of phonetic symbols designed to facilitate linguistic notation.

isolate: A language with no known relatives.

isolating language (or **analytic language**): A language in which the grammatical relationships between words in a sentence are determined by word order rather than case endings or similar grammatical inflections.

kana: Either of the two Japanese syllabaries (*katakana* and *hiragana*).

kanji: The Japanese term for a borrowed Chinese character that can have reading values in either Japanese or Chinese (or both), based on the pronunciation and meaning of the sign at the time it was first borrowed. See *kun* and *on*.

katakana: Japanese syllabary used to spell names in foreign languages (not including Chinese) and for onomatopoeia, interjections, and emphasis.

kun (or *kun'yomi*): The value of a *kanji* based on the pronunciation of a native Japanese word that closely approximated its meaning when first introduced. Some *kanji* have multiple *kun* readings; others, none at all.

ligature: A logogram resulting from the fixed combination of two or more phonetic signs. For example, the ampersand sign (&) results from the combination of *E* and *t* (Latin *et*, "and").

Linear A: An undeciphered logosyllabic script found mostly on Crete, Thera, and other Cycladic islands, dating to c. 1800–1450 B.C.

Linear B (also **Mycenaean script**): Logosyllabic script recording the Mycenaean Greek language, mostly known from Crete and mainland Greece and dating to c. 1450–1200 B.C. Deciphered by Michael Ventris in 1952.

logogram (or **logograph**, **lexical sign**): Literally a "word sign," a logogram denotes a specific word and its meaning in an underlying language.

logoconsonantal script: A writing system composed of logograms and consonantal signs.

logographic: Of or relating to logograms. (The adjectival form of the word logogram.)

logographic script: A writing system composed entirely of logograms. A conceptual category only because there are no known writing systems without phonetic signs.

logophonetic script: A writing system composed of logograms and phonetic signs (without specifying whether the latter are consonantal, alphabetic, or syllabic).

logosyllabic script (or **logosyllabary**): A writing system composed of logograms and syllabic signs, such as Mayan and Aztec writing.

manner of articulation: Refers to the way in which air pressure, vocal cords, and other features help to produce a sound (e.g., plosive, fricative, nasal).

man'yogana: The early Chinese characters used in 5th-century Japan for their sound values alone, eventually giving rise to the two *kana* syllabaries.

Mayan: Refers to a large group of related languages and their speakers in Mexico and Central America. By convention, *Maya* refers to the people and their culture, whereas *Mayan* specifically refers to language.

Mesopotamia: The land between the Tigris and Euphrates rivers in present-day Iraq; a rich alluvial plain sometimes called the "fertile crescent." Mesopotamia was the site of the ancient civilizations of Akkad, Assyria, Babylonia, Elam, and Sumer.

mixed script: A general term for a logophonetic script.

monogenesis: The theory that writing was invented only once (usually in Mesopotamia), after which it diffused to all later groups.

morpheme: The smallest indivisible unit of meaning in a language. The English word *tapping* is composed of two morphemes: the verbal root *tap* and the bound morpheme *-ing*, indicating a participle or gerund. (The doubled *p* is an orthographic device cueing the short vowel of *tap* in *tapping*, rather than the historic long vowel of *tape* in *taping*.)

Nahuatl: The language of the Aztecs and many of their neighbors in Central Mexico. A member of the widespread Uto-Aztecan language family and the language recorded in the Aztec script.

nasal: Refers to a voiced sound made by resonating the nasal cavity, such as *m*, *n*, and ŋ (the consonant known as *engma* and written *-ng* in the English word *sing*).

numeral (or **numeric sign**): A sign for a number, such as the Arabic numerals 1, 2, and 3.

obelisk: A monumental stone pillar, usually with a square cross section and a pyramidal apex.

on (or ***on'yomi***): The value of a *kanji* based on the Japanese pronunciation of its Chinese reading when first introduced. Some *kanji* have multiple *on* readings, whereas those invented more recently in Japan usually have none.

onomastics: The field of study concerning the origin, construction, and meaning of names.

palatal: A sound made with the hard palate, such as *ch* ([č]) or *sh* ([š]). The linguistic term *palatalization* applies to the change of a velar sound, such as *k*, into č or š.

papyrus: A tall, aquatic sedge (*Cyperus papyrus*), native to central Africa and the Nile valley and from which the earliest paper was made. Early

Semitic and Greek words for this plant are the sources of the English words *paper*, *bible*, and *bibliography*.

pars pro toto: A visual abbreviation common to hieroglyphic writing systems, whereby a distinctive part of a sign can stand for the whole, as the Maya **ka** syllable (a fish or just its fins); the Aztec **ITZ** sign, "obsidian" (an obsidian-edged weapon or just its blade); and the Egyptian **rʻ** sign, "sun" (the god Horus with solar disk headdress or just the disk).

pharyngeal: A sound produced by articulating the root of the tongue with the pharynx, as in the Semitic consonant *ʼayin*.

phoneme: A sound that, in contrast with other sounds, contributes to the set of meaningful phonetic contrasts in a given language. By convention, linguists enclose phonemes in forward slashes (e.g., /p/) to distinguish them from mere phonetic sounds, conventionally enclosed in square brackets (e.g., [p]). In English /b/ and /p/ are different phonemes because *bit* and *pit* contrast meaningfully. In Korean, 빛 ("light") can be pronounced either [bit] or [pit]; thus, [b] and [p] do not contrast and are not distinct phonemes.

phonetic sign (or **phonogram**): A sign for an abstract sequence of sound. Phonetic signs do not carry meaning and come in numerous formal varieties, including consonants (C), vowels (V), consonant groups (CC and CCC), consonant-vowel groups (CV), vowel-consonant groups (VC), and even consonant-vowel-consonant groups (CVC). But no script has all of these forms. For instance, Egyptian phonetic signs are only C, CC, and CCC (e.g., **n**, **nb**, and **nfr**) and Maya phonetic signs are only V and CV (e.g., **a** and **ka**).

phonetic complement: A phonetic sign used to clarify the reading of an associated logogram, indicating (and at least partially reiterating) its reading. Often, this is done to provide a grammatical inflection to a verb root provided by the logogram, as in Japanese and Mayan.

phonetic-semantic sign: Refers to the most common kind of Chinese character, which combines a semantic sign indicating the semantic class of a word with a phonetic sign indicating its pronunciation (minus tone).

pictography (also **picture writing**): A system of nonlinguistic graphic communication conveying information through imagery and context. Most writing systems have signs that originated pictographically, but this says nothing about the function of those signs in a writing system, which will always be phonetic, logographic, or semantic. Grammatologists have retired the term *pictogram* (or *pictograph*) as a sign type.

picture biscript: A close association between text and image (as in a caption), whereby the image provides a helpful constraint on the meaning of the text.

Pinyin: The standard system of Romanized spelling for transliterating Chinese writing; from Mandarin 拼音, *pīn-yīn*, literally "spell-sound."

plosive (also **stop**): A consonant sound made by briefly building up pressure behind the point of articulation and then releasing it, as in *p*, *b*, and *k*. Contrast with **fricative**.

place (or **point) of articulation**: Refers to the location in the mouth where a sound is made or the parts of the mouth responsible for a sound (e.g., bilabial, dental, alveolar, palatal, velar, glottal).

polygenesis: The theory that writing was independently invented several times in different parts of the world.

polyvalent sign (or **homograph**): A sign with two or more reading values, such as most Japanese *kanji* and many cuneiform logograms.

proper name (also **proper noun** or **rigid designator**): A name used for a specific person, place, or thing. In English, proper names always receive initial capital letters.

Proto-Sinaitic: The oldest known ancestor of the alphabet, a pictorial abjad dating to the mid-19th century B.C. and currently attested in the southwest Sinai Peninsula and Middle Egypt.

radical: See **semantic sign**.

rebus: A principle of logophonetic scripts whereby a logogram is used for its phonetic value to signal a homophonous word (e.g., Mayan **BAAH**, "gopher," used to write *baah*, "head").

relational unit (or **relational sign**): A type of logogram in which two preexisting signs are combined to convey a third concept, as when the Chinese logogram 日, **rì** ("sun"), and 月, **yuè** ("moon"), combine to form 明, **míng** ("bright").

representational sign (also **iconic sign**): A type of logogram in which the form or orientation of the sign visually signals the word referred to, such as the Chinese signs for the numbers 一 1, 二 2, and 三 3.

romaji: Japanese term for the Roman alphabet borrowed to transliterate *kanji*, *hiragana*, and *katakana*.

rune (also **runic**): The alphabet adopted by Germanic peoples in the 2nd century A.D. The early and continental variants are known as the *fuþark* (after the first six signs), whereas the later Anglo-Saxon derivation is known as the *fuþorc* (as the result of sound change in the fourth sign).

semantic sign (also **determinative**, **taxon**, or **radical**): A sign without a phonetic value of its own, but which signals the semantic class to which an associated logogram or group of phonetic signs belongs. What Linear B scholars traditionally call an ideogram is, thus, a semantic sign.

Semitic: A large family of languages spoken in the Middle East and Ethiopia, including Arabic, Hebrew, Aramaic, and the now-extinct Babylonian. Best known for its three-consonant word roots, e.g., Arabic KTB ("write"), giving *kataba* ("he wrote"), *maktab* ("office"), and so on. The common ancestor of these languages is known as Proto-Semitic.

shorthand: A method of rapid writing by means of abbreviation and phonetic signs, especially for taking dictation. The most popular systems were designed by Isaac Pitman and John R. Gregg in the late 19th century; both are featural scripts.

sign (or **grapheme**): An irreducible graphic unit of a script possessing its own reading value. The major sign types are logograms, phonetic signs, semantic signs, diacritics, and numerals.

Sino-Tibetan: A language family that includes Chinese, Tibetan, and many other languages of southern and southeast Asia. Tonal contrasts are a common feature of these languages.

stela (pl. **stelae**): A common format for carved monuments, the stela is a freestanding, dressed stone slab erected in a public space to commemorate important events.

syllabic sign (or **syllabogram**): A phonetic sign representing a pronounceable syllable and, therefore, always including a vowel either alone or preceded and/or followed by a consonant. For example, the Maya signs **a** and **ka** are syllabic signs, as are the Aztec signs **o**, **to**, and **ol**.

syllabary: A writing system composed, in whole or in part, of syllabic signs. The Inuktitut syllabary is composed entirely of syllabic signs, but most syllabaries are part of more complex scripts. Examples of these include Linear B (with its many semantic signs), Old Persian (with a few logograms), Mayan (with hundreds of logograms), and Japanese (with two syllabaries and thousands of logograms).

taxon: See **semantic sign**.

Tengwar (also **Tîw**): A calligraphic featural script invented by J.R.R. Tolkien.

theonym: Proper name referring to a god.

thorn (also **þorn**): Name of the first letter in the runic alphabets, þ, standing for the voiced and unvoiced dental fricative *th*.

tone: Refers to a phonemic pitch carried by vowels, as in Chinese and other Sino-Tibetan languages. Tone usually results from compensation for the loss of earlier consonants.

toponym: Proper name referring to a place.

velar: A sound made with the velum or soft palate, such as *k*.

vocalic sign: A sign representing a vowel.

voicing: Refers to the vibration of the vocal cords in the production of various sounds, such as vowels and the voiced consonants *b*, *d*, and *g*.

vowel: A speech sound produced by a relatively open vocal tract, with vibration of the vocal cords but without audible friction. Usually forms the nucleus of a syllable. Depending on where they are made in the mouth, vowels can be classified as high (*i*, *u*), mid (*e*, *o*), low (*a*), front (*e*, *i*), and back (*o*, *u*). Thus, *i* is high front vowel; *o* a mid back one.

word sign: see **logogram**.

writing: A system of graphic marks representing the sounds and words of spoken language. As DeFrancis noted: "writing is visible speech."

Bibliography

Abercrombie, David. *Studies in Phonetics and Linguistics*. London: Oxford University Press, 1965. General introduction to phonetics, with an accessible introduction to Lodwick's universal alphabet (pp. 46–54).

Adkins, Lesley. *Empires of the Plain: Henry Rawlinson and the Lost Languages of Babylon*. New York: St. Martin's Press, 2003. Popular account of Rawlinson's work on the Behistun monument and the decipherment of Babylonian cuneiform.

Adkins, Lesley, and Roy Adkins. *The Keys of Egypt: The Race to Read the Hieroglyphs*. London: HarperCollins, 2009. An overview of the race between Champollion and Young to decipher Egyptian hieroglyphs. See also Robinson, 2012.

————. *Archaeological Illustration*. New York: Cambridge University Press, 2009. An introduction to the principles and methods of archaeological illustration.

Antonsen, Elmer H. "The Runes: The Earliest Germanic Writing System." In *The Origins of Writing*, edited by W. M. Senner, pp. 137–158. Omaha: University of Nebraska Press, 1989. On the origins of the runes. See also Williams, 1996, 2004.

Aubin, Joseph Marius Alexis. *Mémoires sur la peinture didactique et l'écriture figurative des anciens Mexicains*. Paris, 1849. Aubin's methods and results in the decipherment of Aztec hieroglyphic writing. Reprinted in 1885 as *Mission Scientifique au Mexique et dans l'Amerique Centrale, Recherches Historiques et Archéologiques, Première Partie: Histoire*, edited by E. T. Hamy, pp. 1–106, Paris.

Bagley, Robert W. "Anyang Writing and the Origin of the Chinese Writing System." In *The First Writing: Script Invention as History and Process*, edited by S. Houston, pp. 190–249. New York: Cambridge University Press, 2004. On the origins and development of Chinese characters.

Baines, John, John Bennet, and Stephen D. Houston, eds. *The Disappearance of Writing Systems: Perspectives on Literacy and Communication*. London: Equinox, 2008. Edited volume exploring script death as a comparative phenomenon. The authors find little to unite different episodes of script death, suggesting the prevalence of social, political, and economic factors.

Banta, Melissa, Curtis M. Hinsley, and J. Kathryn O'Donnell. *From Site to Sight: Anthropology, Photography and the Power of Imagery*. Cambridge: Peabody Museum Press, 1986. Catalog of an exhibit at the Peabody Museum, Harvard University, exploring the ways in which anthropologists have used photography to pursue their research since the late 19th century.

Blackman, Aylward M. *The Rock Tombs of Meir*. London: Egypt Exploration Fund, 1914–1953. Six volumes detailing Blackman's excavations and finds in the Meir tombs of Upper Egypt.

Bodel, John. "Paragrams, Punctuation, and System in Ancient Roman Script." In *The Shape of Script: How and Why Writing Systems Change*, edited by S. Houston, pp. 65–92. Santa Fe, NM: School for Advanced Research Press, 2012. A useful discussion of the origins and development of various paratextual features of the Roman alphabet, such as punctuation and other nonalphabetical symbols.

Bond, Sarah. "Erasing the Face of History." *The New York Times*, May 14, 2011. Discusses the Cairo court's *damnatio memoriae* of former Egyptian president Ḥusnī Mubārak. Available online at http://www.nytimes.com/2011/05/15/opinion/15bond.html.

Bonfante, Giuliano, and Larissa Bonfante. *The Etruscan Language: An Introduction*. 2nd ed. Manchester: Manchester University Press, 2003. Detailed discussion of what can be reconstructed and inferred about the Etruscan language from texts and Latin glosses.

Bonfante, Larissa. *Etruscan*. Reading the Past series. London: British Museum, 1990. An accessible introduction to the Etruscan script and language.

Boone, Elizabeth H., and Walter D. Mignolo. *Writing without Words: Alternative Literacies in Mesoamerica and the Andes*. Durham, NC: Duke University Press, 1994. This edited volume presents an argument for a broader definition of writing, encompassing all graphic communication systems.

Booth, Arthur John. *The Discovery and Decipherment of the Trilingual Cuneiform Inscriptions*. New York: Longmans, Green, and Company, 1902. Classic study of the cuneiform texts of the Achaemenid era.

Bowman, Alan K. *Life and Letters on the Roman Frontier: Vindolanda and Its People*. New York: Routledge, 1994. Accessible presentation of the early Roman letters from the British frontier and their bearing on society, politics, and economy.

Campbell, Lyle. *Historical Linguistics: An Introduction*. 3rd ed. New York: Cambridge University Press, 2013. Still the best introduction to the comparative method of linguistic reconstruction, now with a broader treatment of philology, including some discussion of the origins and development of Mayan hieroglyphic writing.

Chadwick, John. *Linear B and Related Scripts*. Reading the Past series. London: British Museum, 1987. Accessible introduction to the Cretan and Cypriotic scripts.

———. *The Decipherment of Linear B*. New York: Cambridge University Press, 1958. Detailed account of Ventris's decipherment of the Mycenaean script.

Champollion, Jean-François. *Lettre à M. Dacier ... relative a l'alphabet des hieroglyphes phonétiques*. Paris: Chez Firmin Didot Père et Fils, 1822. Champollion's decipherment of Egyptian hieroglyphic writing, presented in his own words.

———. *Précis du système hiéroglyphique des anciens Égyptiens*. Strasbourg and London: Chez Treuttel et Würtz, 1824. A more ample account of Champollion's decipherment.

———. *Grammaire Égyptienne, ou principes généraux de l'écriture sacrée Égyptienne*. Paris: Typographie de Firmin Didot Fréres, 1836. Champollion's grammar of Egyptian hieroglyphic writing, published posthumously by his brother.

Chiera, Edward. *They Wrote on Clay: The Babylonian Tablets Speak Today*. Chicago: University of Chicago Press, 1938. This slim, early survey of the contents and significance of the cuneiform tablets has yet to be superseded for its accessibility to the average reader.

Christin, Anne-Marie, ed. *Histoire de l'écriture: de l'idéogramme au multimedia*. Paris: Flammarion, 2001. Contains numerous summaries of writing systems and graphic communication systems, with ample sections on the development of the alphabet in the 17th and 18th centuries, though the articles on the Mayan and Aztec scripts are outdated and misleading. Published in English translation as *A History of Writing: From Hieroglyph to Multimedia*, 2002.

Coe, Michael D. *Breaking the Maya Code*. Rev. ed. New York: Thames and Hudson, 1999. An absorbing account of Knorosov's decipherment. Coe's treatment of the history of writing and decipherment in chapter 1, "The Word Made Visible" (pp. 13–45), is both accessible and perceptive.

Coe, Michael D., and Mark Van Stone. *Reading the Maya Glyphs*. 2nd ed. New York: Thames and Hudson, 2005. A popular introduction to Mayan hieroglyphs for beginners.

Collier, Mark, and Bill Manley. *How to Read Egyptian Hieroglyphs: A Step-by-Step Guide to Teach Yourself*. Rev. ed. Berkeley: University of California Press, 2003. An in-depth introduction to Egyptian hieroglyphs.

Common Core State Standards Initiative. *Common Core State Standards for English Language Arts and Literacy*. Washington DC: National Governors Association (NGA) Center for Best Practices, Council of Chief State School Officers (CCSSO), 2010. The complete proposal for new educational guidelines put forward by the CCSSO and NGA in 2010, now adopted by

45 states, and no longer mandating the teaching of cursive handwriting. Available online at http://www.corestandards.org.

Cook, B. F. *Greek Inscriptions*. Reading the Past series. London: British Museum, 1987. Accessible introduction to the origins and development of the Greek alphabet, as well as to Greek epigraphy.

Crossman, William. *VIVO [Voice-In/Voice-Out]: The Coming Age of Talking Computers*. Oakland, CA: Regent Press, 2004. Crossman predicts a future without writing or reading.

Crystal, David. *Txtng: The Gr8 Db8*. New York: Oxford University Press, 2009. An engaging look at the peculiar orthographic habits of teenagers and the fact that they don't spell the end of either the English language or our writing system.

Dahm, Murray K. "Roman Frontier Signalling and the Order of the Futhark." *The Journal of Indo-European Studies* 39(1): 1–12, 2011. Intriguing contribution to the study of runic origins, arguing that the inexplicable order of the fuþark may stem from early Roman conventions for fire signaling. See also Williams, 1996, 2004.

Daniels, Peter T. "Fundamentals of Grammatology." *Journal of the American Oriental Society* 110(4): 727–731, 1990. Excellent short summary of the field of comparative writing.

Daniels, Peter T., and William Bright, eds. *The World's Writing Systems*. New York: Oxford University Press, 1996. Contains numerous capable summaries of scripts, particularly those of Southeast Asia, with the caveat that the articles on the Mesoamerican scripts are superficial and in some respects outdated.

Darnell, J. C., F. W. Dobbs-Allsopp, M. J. Lundberg, P. K. McCarter, and B. Zuckerman. "Two Early Alphabetic Inscriptions from Wadi el-Ḥôl: New Evidence for the Origin of the Alphabet from the Western Desert of Egypt." *Annual of the American Schools of Oriental Research* 59, pp. 63–124.

Boston: ASOR, 2005. Publication of the Proto-Sinaitic inscriptions from the Wadi el-Ḥôl.

Darwin, Charles. *On the Origin of Species by Means of Natural Selection, or the Preservation of Favoured Races in the Struggle for Life.* London: John Murray, 1859. The book that changed everything and introduced a rigorous approach to the comparative study of organisms in order to trace their descent.

DeFrancis, John. *The Chinese Language: Fact and Fantasy.* Honolulu: University of Hawaii Press, 1984. Outlines the nature of the Chinese languages in an accessible way.

———. *Visible Speech: The Diverse Oneness of Writing Systems.* Honolulu: University of Hawaii Press, 1989. This book by a well-regarded Sinologist and specialist in Chinese languages and writing demonstrates that all writing systems record language.

———. "The Ideographic Myth." In *Difficult Characters: Interdisciplinary Studies of Chinese and Japanese Writing*, edited by M. S. Erbaugh, pp. 1–20. Columbus: Ohio State University, 2002. Dispels the ideographic fallacy in the context of Chinese writing.

Diringer, David. *The Hand-Produced Book.* London: Hutchinson's Scientific and Technical Publications, 1953. This classic work is now somewhat outdated but still repays close reading. It was reprinted by Dover Books in 1982 and 2011 as *The Book before Printing: Ancient, Medieval and Oriental.*

———. *The Alphabet: A Key to the History of Mankind.* 3rd ed. 2 vols. New York: Funk & Wagnalls, 1968. A survey of the origins, development, and relationships of the world's alphabets, though now outdated in many specifics.

Doumas, Christos G. *Thera: Pompeii of the Ancient Aegean. Excavations at Akrotiri, 1967–1979.* New York: Thames and Hudson, 1983. Popular introduction to Minoan archaeology by one of the excavators of Thera.

Elliott, Ralph W. V. *Runes: An Introduction.* 2nd ed. Manchester: Manchester University Press, 1989. This classic work was first published in 1959 and remains a solid introduction to the subject, even though superseded in some respects by Page (1987, 1999).

Fane, Diane. "Reproducing the Pre-Columbian Past: Casts and Models in Exhibitions of Ancient America, 1824–1935." In *Collecting the Past*, edited by E. Boone, pp. 141–176. Washington DC: Dumbarton Oaks, 1993. Discusses the pros and cons of casts in recording ancient monuments.

Fash, Barbara. "Cast Aside: Revisiting the Plaster Cast Collections from Mesoamerica." *Visual Resources* 20(1): 3-17, 2004. Excellent discussion of the challenges and rewards of curating monument casts.

Fazzini, Richard A., James F. Romano, and Madeline E. Cody. *Art for Eternity: Masterworks from Ancient Egypt.* New York: Brooklyn Museum of Art, 1999. Catalog of 100 highlights from the BMA's Egyptian collection, including the fragmentary relief panel of Tuthmosis III (p. 79).

Federman, Mark. "What Is the Meaning of 'The Medium Is the Message'?" 2004. Short article putting McLuhan's famous expression in context. Available online at: http://individual.utoronto.ca/markfederman/article_ mediumisthemessage.htm.

Fox, Margalit. "Alice E. Kober, 43; Lost to History No More." *The New York Times*, May 12, 2013. Reflections on the life and achievement of Alice Kober. Available online at: http://www.nytimes.com/2013/05/12/sunday-review/alice-e-kober-43-lost-to-history-no-more.html.

Friedrich, Johannes. *Entzifferung verschollener Schriften und Sprachen.* Berlin: Springer-Verlag, 1954. Translated into English under the title *Extinct Languages* (New York: Philosophical Library, 1957), this is a classic discussion of the principles and methodology of decipherment by a true expert.

Gardiner, A. H. *Egyptian Grammar: Being an Introduction to the Study of Hieroglyphs*. 3rd ed. London: Oxford University Press, 1957. The standard reference work on Egyptian hieroglyphic grammar.

Gelb, Ignace J. *A Study of Writing: The Foundations of Grammatology*. Chicago: University of Chicago Press, 1952. Gelb's classic initiated the study of comparative writing and provided many of the technical terms the field still uses today, though it's not without its defects. A second, revised edition was issued in 1963. See chapter 10 for Gelb's view of the future of writing as he saw it more than 60 years ago.

Geller, Marckham. "The Last Wedge." *Zeitschrift für Assyriologie und vorderasiatische Archäologie* 86: 43–95, 1997. On the last Akkadian cuneiform inscription, dating to the late 1st century A.D.

Goldwasser, Orly. "How the Alphabet Was Born from Hieroglyphs." *Biblical Archaeology Review* 36(2): 40–53, 2010. Presents Goldwasser's theory of the formal derivation of Proto-Sinaitic signs from Egyptian hieroglyphs.

Goody, Jack, and Ian P. Watt. "The Consequences of Literacy." *Comparative Studies in Society and History* 5: 304–345, 1963. Influential essay arguing that the invention of the alphabet was a precondition for the development of logic and rationality, abstract thinking, and classification. Reprinted in E. R. Kintgen et al., eds., *Perspectives on Literacy* (1988), pp. 3–27.

Gordon, Cyrus H. *Forgotten Scripts: Their Ongoing Discovery and Decipherment*. Rev. ed. New York: Basic Books, 1982. Accessible comparative discussion of the decipherments of several Old World scripts.

Griffith, Francis Llewellyn. "Meroitic Inscriptions." In *Arieka, Eckley B. Coxe Junior Expedition to Nubia*, vol. I, edited by D. Randall-MacIver and C. Leonard Woolley, pp. 43–54. Oxford, 1909. Presents Griffith's initial decipherment of Meroïtic.

Healey, John F. *The Early Alphabet*. Reading the Past series. London: British Museum Press, 1990. Accessible introduction to the origins and development of the alphabet.

Hill, Archibald A. "The Typology of Writing Systems." In *Papers in Linguistics in Honor of Léon Dostert*, edited by W. M. Austin, pp. 92–99. The Hague: Mouton, 1967. Useful discussion of script typology. See also Daniels, 1990.

Hincks, Edward. "On the Three Kinds of Persepolitan Writing and on the Babylonian Lapidary Characters." *Transactions of the Royal Irish Academy* 21: 233–248, 1848. Hincks's analysis of the three Achaemenid-era scripts.

Homer. *The Iliad*. Rev. ed. Translated by E. V. Rieu. London: Penguin Books, 2003. Homer's song of the wrath of Achilles and the downfall of Troy.

———. *The Odyssey*. Translated by W. Shewring. New York: Oxford University Press, 2008. Homer's song of Odysseus's long journey home.

Houston, Stephen D, ed. *The First Writing: Script Invention as History and Process*. New York: Cambridge University Press, 2004. Edited volume of articles exploring the origins of writing.

———, ed. *The Shape of Script: How and Why Writing Systems Change*. Santa Fe, NM: School for Advanced Research Press, 2012. Edited volume of articles exploring script paleography and development.

Jones, William. "Third Anniversary Discourse." *Asiatic Researches* 1: 415–431, 1788. William Jones's influential observations on the similarity of Latin, Greek, and Sanskrit. Delivered to the Asiatic Society in Calcutta, 1786.

Kahn, David. *The Codebreakers: The Story of Secret Writing*. Rev. ed. New York: Scribner, 1996. Well-illustrated and accessible account of cryptography.

Kamrin, Janice. *Ancient Egyptian Hieroglyphs: A Practical Guide.* New York: Harry N. Abrams, 2004. A popular introduction to Egyptian hieroglyphs for beginners.

Kent, R. G. *Old Persian: Grammar, Texts, Lexicon.* 2nd ed. New Haven: American Oriental Society, 1953. Detailed analysis of the Old Persian language as revealed in the texts of Persepolis and elsewhere.

Kober, Alice E. "Inflection in Linear Class B: 1—Declension." *American Journal of Archaeology* 50(2): 268–276, 1946. Kober's evidence for grammatical endings in Linear B spellings and their implications for shared consonants and vowels between signs.

———. "The Minoan Scripts: Facts and Theory." *The American Journal of Archaeology.* 52(1): 82–103, 1948. Early overview of the Cretan and Cypriotic scripts.

———. "'Total' in Minoan (Linear Class B)." *Archiv Orientálni* 17(2): 386–398, 1949. Kober's evidence for the indication of gender in variable spellings of the Linear B word for "total" (*to-so* and *to-sa*).

Kuhrt, Amélie. *The Persian Empire: A Corpus of Sources from the Achaemenid Period.* New York: Routledge, 2007. Accessible account of the Achaemenid Empire from historical sources.

Lacadena, Alfonso. "A Nahuatl Syllabary." *The PARI Journal* 8(4): 23, 2008. First publication of Lacadena's grid of Aztec phonetic signs. Available online at: http://www.mesoweb.com/pari/journal/archive/PARI0804.pdf.

———. "Regional Scribal Traditions: Methodological Implications for the Decipherment of Nahuatl Writing." *The PARI Journal* 8(4): 1–22, 2008. Establishes the rationale for considering all examples of Aztec writing, whatever their region or time period, in pursuing its decipherment. Available online at: http://www.mesoweb.com/pari/journal/archive/PARI0804.pdf.

Lepsius, Richard. "*Lettre à M. le Professeur H. Rosellini ... sur l'alphabet hiéroglyphique.*" *Annali dell'Instituto di corrispondenza archeologica* 9: 5–100. Rome, 1837. In this key paper, Lepsius established that not all Egyptian phonetic signs conveyed single consonants. There were also biliterals (with two consonants, such as **mn**) and triliterals (with three consonants, such as **nfr**).

Lodwick, Francis. "An Essay Towards an Universal Alphabet." *Philosophical Transactions* 16: 126–137, 1686. Lodwick's own presentation of his invented alphabet, including his rationale for the invention.

Logan, Robert K. *The Alphabet Effect: The Impact of the Phonetic Alphabet on the Development of Western Civilization*. New York: William Morrow, 1986. Argues that the alphabet played "a particularly dynamic role" in the codification of law, monotheism, abstract theoretical science, formal logic, and individualism. See also Goody and Watt, 1963.

Loprieno, Antonio. *Ancient Egyptian: A Linguistic Introduction*. New York: Cambridge University Press, 1995. Detailed look at the phonology (sound system) and morphology (grammar) of ancient Egyptian.

Lurie, David B. "The Development of Writing in Japan." In *The Shape of Script: How and Why Writing Systems Change*, edited by S. Houston, pp. 159–185. Santa Fe, NM: School for Advanced Research Press, 2012. A wide-ranging discussion of the historical development of the world's most complicated writing system.

MacMahon, M. K. C. "Henry Sweet's System of Shorthand." In *Towards a History of Phonetics*, edited by R. E. Asher and E. Henderson, pp. 265–281. Edinburgh: Edinburgh University Press, 1981. Useful historical discussion of Sweet's shorthand and comparison with competing systems.

Malik, Khalid. *Summary Human Development Report, 2013. The Rise of the South: Human Progress in a Diverse World*. New York: United Nations Development Programme, 2013. The UN report on human development for 2013, including comparative metrics for education and literacy. Available online at: http://hdr.undp.org/en/reports/global/hdr2013/.

Mallery, Garrick. *Pictographs of the North American Indians: A Preliminary Paper*. Fourth Annual Report of the Bureau of Ethnology. Washington, DC: Smithsonian Institution, 1887. Detailed overview of the graphic communication systems of the Plains Indians, including anecdotal accounts and numerous illustrations.

Mann, Charles C. "Cracking the Khipu Code." *Science* 300(5626): 1650–1651, 2003. Usefully sets out the arguments, pro and con, for the khipu as a kind of writing system.

Marinatos, Spyridon. "The Volcanic Destruction of Minoan Crete." *Antiquity* 13(52): 425–439, 1939. Accessible overview of the eruption of Thera from the first archaeologist to excavate Akrotiri.

McLuhan, Marshall. *The Gutenberg Galaxy: The Making of Typographic Man.* New York: Routledge, 1962. Explores the effects of the printing press and other mass media on civilization. Introduced the term *global village.*

———. *Understanding Media: The Extensions of Man.* New York: McGraw-Hill, 1964. Proposal that media themselves, rather than just content, form a subject of study. Introduced McLuhan's celebrated axiom "The medium is the message."

Melikian, Souren. "The Mysteries of Meroe." *The New York Times*, May 21, 2010. Review of the exhibit *Méroé, un empire sur le Nil* at the Louvre, Paris. Includes some discussion of the vase of Sotades of Athens discovered at Meroë. Available online at: http://www.nytimes.com/2010/05/22/arts/22iht-melik22.html.

Metzger, Bruce M. "When Did Scribes Begin to Use Writing Desks?" In *Historical and Literary Studies: Pagan, Jewish, and Christian.* Grand Rapids, MI: Eerdmans, 1968. Useful contribution to the question of chronology in the abandonment of papyrus scrolls for parchment codices.

Meyerson, Daniel. *The Linguist and the Emperor: Napoleon and Champollion's Quest to Decipher the Rosetta Stone.* New York: Ballantine Books, 2004. Popular account of the influence of Napoleonic-era politics on Champollion's decipherment of Egyptian.

Miller, R. A. *The Japanese Language.* Chicago: University of Chicago Press, 1967. General introduction to the history and structure of Japanese.

Miyake, Marc Hideo. *Old Japanese: A Phonetic Reconstruction*. New York: Routledge, 2003. Useful reconstruction of the Japanese language at the time of the earliest documents, c. 8th century A.D.

Moltke, Erik. *Runes and Their Origin: Denmark and Elsewhere*. Translated by P. G. Foote. Copenhagen: National Museum of Denmark, 1985. Classic study of runic origins.

Moore, Oliver. *Chinese*. Reading the Past series. London: British Museum Press, 2000. Accessible introduction to the origins and development of Chinese writing.

Murray, Oswyn. "Greek Historians." In *The Oxford History of the Classical World*, edited by J. Boardman, J. Griffin, and O. Murray, pp. 188–192. New York: Oxford University Press, 1986. Useful discussion and comparison of Herodotus and other early Greek historians.

Nicholson, H. B. "Phoneticism in the Late Pre-Hispanic Central Mexican Writing System." In *Mesoamerican Writing Systems: A Conference at Dumbarton Oaks, October 30th and 31st, 1971*, edited by E. Benson, pp. 1–46. Washington DC: Dumbarton Oaks, 1973. Perceptive analysis of phonetic complementation in examples of Precolumbian Aztec hieroglyphic writing.

Niebuhr, Carsten. *Reisebeschreibung nach Arabien und andern umliegenden Ländern*. 2 vols. Copenhagen: Nicolaus Moeller, 1774–1778. Classic account of the author's rediscovery and recording of the cuneiform inscriptions of Persepolis. Published in an abridged English translation by Robert Heron, *Travels through Arabia, and Other Countries in the East Performed by M. Niebuhr* (Edinburgh, 1792).

Nuttall, Zelia. "On the Complementary Signs of the Mexican Graphic System." Appendix to *Standard or Head-dress? An Historical Essay on a Relic of Ancient Mexico*. Archaeological and Ethnological Papers of the Peabody Museum 1(1): 49–52. Cambridge, MA: Peabody Museum, 1888. Nuttall was the first to observe the principle of phonetic complementation in Aztec hieroglyphic writing. Recently reprinted in *The PARI Journal* 8(4):

46–48, 2008. Available online at: http://www.mesoweb.com/pari/journal/archive/PARI0804.pdf.

Oates, Joan, ed. Special issue: Early Writing Systems. *World Archaeology* 17(3): 307–460, 1986. Useful compilation of articles on the origins of several Old World writing systems.

Page, Raymond I. *An Introduction to English Runes*. 2nd ed. Woodbridge, Suffolk, UK: Boydell Press, 1999. Authoritative introduction to the Anglo-Saxon runes.

———. *Runes*. Reading the Past series. London: British Museum Press, 1987. Accessible introduction to the origins and development of the runes.

———. *Runes and Runic Inscriptions. Collected Essays on Anglo-Saxon and Viking Runes*. Woodbridge, Suffolk, UK: Boydell Press, 1995. Detailed discussions of many runic topics.

Pallottino, Massimo. *The Etruscans*. Rev. ed. London: Penguin Books, 1975. Useful survey of Etruscan archaeology, history, and culture.

Parkinson, Richard B. *The Rosetta Stone*. London: British Museum Press, 2005. Detailed history and discussion of the iconic artifact.

Pellegrino, Charles. *Unearthing Atlantis: An Archaeological Odyssey*. New York: Vintage Books, 1991. Popular account of the Thera eruption.

Piper, H. Beam. "Omnilingual." *Astounding Science Fiction*. February 1957. Fascinating science fiction tale asking whether an ancient Martian alphabet might be decipherable even without a known language or bilingual.

Polacco, Patricia, *Thank You, Mr. Falker*. New York: Philomel Books, 1998. Emotional account of one woman's struggle with dyslexia and an extraordinary teacher.

Pope, Maurice. *The Story of Decipherment: From Egyptian Hieroglyphs to Maya Script.* Rev. ed. New York: Thames and Hudson, 1999. Solid comparative account of several key decipherments.

Possehl, Gregory L. *Indus Age: The Writing System.* Philadelphia: University of Pennsylvania Press, 1996. Overview of the Indus script.

Postgate, Nicholas, Tao Wang, and Toby Wilkinson. "The Evidence for Early Writing: Utilitarian or Ceremonial?" *Antiquity* 69: 459–480, 1995. Argues that, despite the better preservation of ceremonial examples of early Chinese writing on bronze vessels and ox scapulae, the earliest records are more likely to have been administrative and written on perishable media.

Quilter, Jeffrey, Marc Zender, Karen Spalding, Régulo Franco, César Gálvez, and Juan Castañeda. "Traces of a Lost Language and Number System Discovered on the North Coast of Peru." *American Anthropologist* 112(3): 357–369, 2010. Discusses a 17th-century document with a previously unknown language written in the Spanish (Roman) alphabet, recently excavated at Magdalena de Cao, Peru. Available online at: http://onlinelibrary.wiley.com/doi/10.1111/j.1548-1433.2010.01245.x/pdf.

Rawlinson, Henry C. "The Persian Cuneiform Inscription at Behistun, Decyphered and Translated; with a Memoir." *Journal of the Royal Asiatic Society* 11: 1–192, 1849. Initial publication of the Behistun inscriptions, with the author's account of the decipherment of Old Persian.

Rilly, Claude. "The Linguistic Position of Meroitic." *Arkamani, Sudan Electronic Journal of Archaeology and Anthropology*, March 2004. Proposed connection between Meroïtic and Nilo-Saharan languages (such as Nubian) on the basis of speculative shared vocabulary. Available online at: http://www.arkamani.org/arkamani–library/meroitic/rilly.htm.

Rilly, Claude, and Alex de Voogt. *The Meroitic Language and Writing System.* New York: Cambridge University Press, 2012. Excellent introduction to the Meroïtic script, with a more detailed pursuit of a Nilo-Saharan connection (see Rilly, 2004).

Roberts, Colin H., and Theodore C. Skeat. *The Birth of the Codex*. New York: Oxford University Press, 1983. Classic account of the connection between Christianity and the demise of the papyrus scroll.

Robinson, Andrew. *Lost Languages: The Enigma of the World's Undeciphered Scripts*. New York: McGraw-Hill, 2002. An excellent, accessible overview of undeciphered writing systems.

———. *The Man Who Deciphered Linear B: The Story of Michael Ventris*. New York: Thames and Hudson, 2002. Detailed account of Ventris's decipherment of the Mycenaean script.

———. *The Story of Writing: Alphabets, Hieroglyphs and Pictographs*. 2nd ed. New York: Thames and Hudson, 2007. Well-illustrated survey of scripts and graphic communication.

———. *The Last Man Who Knew Everything: Thomas Young, the Anonymous Genius Who Proved Newton Wrong and Deciphered the Rosetta Stone, Among Other Surprising Feats*. New York: Plume, 2007. A balanced comparison of Young's and Champollion's contributions to the Egyptian decipherment.

———. *Writing and Script: A Very Short Introduction*. New York: Oxford University Press, 2009. A brief but very readable overview of writing. See chapter 8 for a discussion of media, but note that linguists don't accept the speculative derivation of the word *papyrus* from Egyptian **p3y pr-ꜥ3**, "that which is of Pharaoh" (p. 131).

———. *Cracking the Egyptian Code: The Revolutionary Life of Jean-François Champollion*. New York: Oxford University Press, 2012. A detailed account of Champollion's decipherment of Egyptian hieroglyphs.

Rowan, Kirsty. "Meroitic—An Afroasiatic language?" *SOAS Working Papers in Linguistics* 14: 169–206, 2006. Proposed connection between Meroïtic and Afroasiatic languages (such as Egyptian), largely on the basis of structural features.

Ryan, Donald P. "Papyrus." *The Biblical Archaeologist* 51(3): 132–140, 1988. A truly excellent and very readable short article on the many uses of papyrus in ancient Egypt.

Sacks, David. *Language Visible: Unraveling the Mysteries of Our Alphabet from A to Z.* New York: Broadway Books, 2003. A popular account of the origins and development of the alphabet.

Sampson, Geoffrey. *Writing Systems: A Linguistic Introduction.* Stanford, CA: Stanford University Press, 1985. A linguistic approach to the typology of writing. Includes excellent discussions of the Chinese, Japanese, and Korean scripts. Introduced the term *featural script* (p. 40).

Sandys, John Edwin. *Latin Epigraphy: An Introduction to the Study of Latin Inscriptions.* Cambridge: Cambridge University Press, 1919. Classic introduction to Roman inscriptions.

Sansom, George B. *Japan: A Short Cultural History.* New York: Appleton, 1962. Good introduction to Japanese culture and history.

Schmandt-Besserat, Denise. *Before Writing.* Austin: University of Texas Press, 1992. Argues that clay tokens played an important role in the development of writing in Mesopotamia.

Seeley, Christopher. *A History of Writing in Japan.* Leiden, The Netherlands: Brill, 1991. Useful discussion of the interplay of writing and civilization in Japan.

Shinnie, Peter L. *Meroe: A Civilization of the Sudan.* New York: Thames and Hudson, 1967. Classic discussion of Meroïtic civilization.

Smiles, Sam, and Stephanie Moser, eds. *Envisioning the Past: Archaeology and the Image.* Malden, MA: Wiley-Blackwell, 2005. Discusses how archaeologists have used photography in their research.

Smith, Arden R. "The Alphabet of Rúmil: Documents by J.R.R. Tolkien." *Parma Eldalamberon* 13: 5–89, 2001. Edition of Tolkien's earliest invented alphabet.

———. "Pre-Fëanorian Alphabets, Part I: Documents by J.R.R. Tolkien." *Parma Eldalamberon* 16: 5–51, 2006. Edition of the early invented alphabet that would become Tolkien's Tengwar.

———. "The Quenya Alphabet." *Parma Eldalamberon* 20, 2012. Edition of the invented alphabet just prior to its codification by Tolkien as the familiar Tengwar.

Sperber, Dan. "The Future of Writing." Paper presented at the virtual symposium "text-e," 2002. Comparative anthropological arguments regarding the future of writing in an increasingly digital era. Available online at: http://www.dan.sperber.fr/?p=75.

Steiner, Melanie. *Approaches to Archaeological Illustration: A Handbook.* London: Council for British Archaeology, 2005. Good introduction to the principles and techniques of archaeological illustration.

Steinke, Kyle. "Script Change in Bronze Age China." In *The Shape of Script: How and Why Writing Systems Change*, edited by S. Houston, pp. 135–158. Santa Fe: School for Advanced Research Press, 2012. The development of the early Chinese script.

Stephens, George. *Handbook of the Old-Northern Runic Monuments of Scandinavia and England.* London: Williams and Norgate, 1884. This classic compilation of Germanic runestones is a valuable early resource, but Stephens's translations are not trustworthy.

Stone, Andrea, and Marc Zender. *Reading Maya Art: A Hieroglyphic Guide to Ancient Maya Painting and Sculpture.* New York: Thames and Hudson, 2011. Examines the complex interplay between Mayan art and writing in all time periods.

Strassler, Robert B., ed. *The Landmark Herodotus: The Histories*. Translated by Andrea L. Purvis. New York: Pantheon Books, 2007. Excellent, readable translation.

Stuart, David. "Breaking the Code: Rabbit Story." In *Lost Kingdoms of the Maya*, edited by G. E. Stuart and G. S. Stuart, pp. 170–171. Washington DC: National Geographic Society, 1993. First notice of rare first-person pronouns on a Late Classic Maya vase.

Tierney, John. "Who Should Own the Rosetta Stone?" *The New York Times*, November 16, 2009. Interesting short article on the question of the rightful ownership of such pieces as the iconic stone. Available online at: http://tierneylab.blogs.nytimes.com/2009/11/16/who-should-own-the-rosetta-stone/.

Tolkien, J.R.R. *The Lord of the Rings*. 50th anniversary ed. London: HarperCollins, 2004. Tolkien provides a discussion of his invented alphabets in appendix E, complete with charts.

———. *The Silmarillion*. Edited by C. Tolkien. London: George Allen & Unwin, 1977. An account of the First Age of Middle-earth, including the fictional inventors of Tolkien's *tengwar* and *certar*.

Townsend, Richard F. *The Aztecs*. 3rd ed. New York: Thames and Hudson, 2009. A standard textbook introduction to the Aztecs. See pp. 206–212 for insights from the recent decipherment of Aztec hieroglyphic writing.

Unger, J. Marshall. *Ideogram: Chinese Characters and the Myth of Disembodied Meaning*. Honolulu: University of Hawaii Press, 2004. Important consideration of Chinese script in light of the ever popular ideographic fallacy.

Urton, Gary. *Signs of the Inka Khipu: Binary Coding in the Andean Knotted-String Records*. Austin: University of Texas Press, 2003. An accessible account of the complex numerical records of the Inka khipu, including arguments for a previously unrecognized binary encoding.

Urton, Gary, and Carrie J. Brezine. "Khipu Accounting in Ancient Peru." *Science* 309(5737): 1065–1067, 2005. Discovery of a non-numerical "introductory segment" in some khipu, possibly provenance information. Although these have been referred to as "words" or even "narrative" information in popular accounts, there's still no evidence for phoneticism in these documents.

Ventris, Michael. "King Nestor's Four-Handled Cups: Greek Inventories in the Minoan Script." *Archaeology* 7(1): 15–21, 1954. A popular account of the Pylos tripod tablet and the Linear B decipherment in Ventris's own words.

———. "Work Notes on Minoan Language Research and Other Unedited Papers." Edited by Anna Sacconi. *Incunabula Graeca* 90. Rome: Edizioni dell'Ateneo, 1988. These posthumously published work notes by Michael Ventris detail the various stages of his decipherment of Linear B.

Ventris, Michael, and John Chadwick. "Evidence for Greek Dialect in the Mycenaean Archives." *The Journal of Hellenic Studies* 73: 84–103, 1953. The official publication of the Linear B decipherment.

———. *Documents in Mycenaean Greek*. Cambridge: Cambridge University Press, 1956. A more ample exploration of the structure and orthographic practices of Linear B, with many translated tablets.

Walker, C. B. F. *Cuneiform*. Reading the Past series. London: British Museum Press, 1987. Accessible introduction to the cuneiform scripts, with sign-by-sign readings of several inscriptions in the major cuneiform systems.

Walker, Willard, and James Sarbaugh. "The Early History of the Cherokee Syllabary." *Ethnohistory* 40(1): 70–94, 1993. A historical look at the origin and early development of Sequoyah's Cherokee syllabary.

Webb-Pressler, Margaret. "The Handwriting Is on the Wall." *The Washington Post*, October 11, 2006. Article on the demise of cursive instruction in many public schools. Available online at: http://www.washingtonpost.com/wp-dyn/content/article/2006/10/10/AR2006101001475.html.

Bibliography

Wells, H. G. *A Short History of the World*. London: Cassel & Co., Ltd., 1922. Popular account of the key events of world history from a renowned polymath. Unintentionally revelatory of the social, political, and economic preoccupations of post-Edwardian interbellum England.

Welsby, Derek A. *The Kingdom of Kush: The Napatan and Meroitic Empires*. London: British Museum Press, 1996. Good introduction to the archaeology and history of Nubia.

Wilford, John Noble. "Finds in Egypt Date Alphabet in Earlier Era." *The New York Times*, November 14, 1999. Excellent, accessible article on the Darnells' discovery of Proto-Sinaitic inscriptions at Wadi el-Ḥôl. Available online at: http://www.nytimes.com/1999/11/14/world/finds-in-egypt-date-alphabet-in-earlier-era.html.

Williams, Henrik. "The Origin of the Runes." *Amsterdamer Beiträge zur älteren Germanistik* 45: 211–218, 1996. Argues for a derivation of runes from Roman capitals.

———. "Reasons for Runes." In *The First Writing: Script Invention as History and Process*, edited by S. Houston, pp. 262–273. New York: Cambridge University Press, 2004. Further details of the derivation of runes from Roman capitals.

Yamauchi, Edwin. "Review of *The Birth of the Codex*." *The Journal of Library History* 20(2): 202–204, 1985. Perceptive review of Roberts and Skeat, 1983.

Zauzich, Karl-Theodor. *Hieroglyphs without Mystery: An Introduction to Ancient Egyptian Writing*. Translated by Ann Macy Roth. Austin: University of Texas Press, 1992. Accessible introduction to the Egyptian script, including many translated texts from Tutankhamun's tomb.

Zender, Marc. *Diacritical Marks and Underspelling in the Classic Maya Script: Implications for Decipherment*. M.A. thesis, University of Calgary. Ann Arbor: University Microfilms International, 1999. Detailed study of the orthographic conventions of Mayan hieroglyphic writing, including abbreviation and diacritics. Discussion of the absence of semantic signs.

—————. "One Hundred and Fifty Years of Nahuatl Decipherment." *The PARI Journal* 8(4): 24–37, 2008. An accessible history of the decipherment of Aztec hieroglyphic writing. Available online at: http://www.mesoweb.com/pari/journal/archive/PARI0804.pdf.

—————. "*Baj* 'Hammer' and Related Affective Verbs in Classic Mayan." *The PARI Journal* 11(2): 1–16, 2010. Although this is a technical analysis of a previously unrecognized verb class in Mayan inscriptions, pages 4–5 provide an up-to-date discussion of the abbreviational conventions of Classic Mayan. Available online at: http://www.mesoweb.com/pari/journal/archive/PARI1102.pdf.